TO ALL PARENTS,
THIS IS THE PROGRAM YOU NEED
TO ASSIST YOUR CHILD(REN) IN AQUIRING
A SOUND BASIS FOR READING,
WRITING AND SPELLING SKILLS.

ALICE HORWILL-LEECH

Published by Alice Horwill-Leech

First published 2013

Written by Alice Horwill-Leech
Illustrations by Danielle Tirchett

the moral right of the author has been asserted.

All rights reserved. Without limiting the rights under copyright restricted above, no part of this publication may be reproduced, stored in or introduced into a retrieval system, or transmitted, in any form or by any means (electronic, mechanical, photocopying, recording or otherwise), without the prior written permission of both the copyright owner and the above publisher of this book.

A Cataloguing-in-Publication record is available from the National Library of Australia.

ISBN: 978-1-954753-45-7 (ebk)
    978-1-954753-44-0 (pbk)

Breaking the Sound Barrier

ABOUT THE AUTHOR

Alice-Horwill-Leech is a registered but retired teacher with many years of teaching experience, especially in the literacy field.

Horwill-Leech is a trained primary school teatcher who has taught a wide age range of students, from preparatory grade to year 10 and also mature aged and English as a second language (E.S.L.) students, furthermore she has also assessed literary work of tertiary students.

Additional academic qualifications include Infant Teachers' Certificate, post graduate Diploma in Special Education and a Master of Education degree. Professional development has also been undertaken for Reading Recovery, THRASS (Teaching Handwriting, Reading and Spelling Skills), Cued Articulation and adult literacy.

WHY DID I WRITE THIS MANUAL?

Throughout my teaching career I have had numerous requests for private tutoring by parents who have deemed that their child(ren) need(s) extra assistance for the acquisition of, and improvement in literacy skills.

These requests have also been coupled with questions and statements such as, '**How** can I assist my child to read better'? 'I don't know **how** to help my child? My child seems to be struggling with his/her reading and spelling. Alternatively this manual may be used at adult learning and continuing education centres with students who wish to improve their understanding of the alphabetic principle that underpins our oral and written language.

Over the years, I have therefore undertaken the privilege of private tutoring with many students, but now no longer accept students in this capacity. I however work voluntarily at one of the local schools.

With requests and statements such as these, I determined that there is a genuine need for some form of assistance for parents and caregivers who genuinely wish to help their children. So with this in mind I commenced to document strategies for teaching students how to understand our alphabetic system, thus building a firm **sound** (in more ways than one) foundation on which to build the subsequent literacy skills of reading writing and spelling.

As explained in the manual, phonological and phonemic awareness skills are the auditory (sounding) processes that are the essential prerequisite skills for literacy success.

Best wishes to all teachers and 'teachers' (meaning those who are not qualified as such but still have a teaching role e.g. parents, grandparents etc.) in your special task of promoting literacy skills to your students, and may you reap the ripe fruits of your labour.

IT'S NOT ROCKET SCIENCE!

My grateful thanks to Leanne Kirkman for her untiring and patient work in typesetting the manual and designing the cover. I also sincerely thank Danielle Tirchett for her time and patience creating all illustrations through-out the text. Also I express my appreciation to Kim Hanlon (CEO, Inglewood Community Resource Centre) for all her technical support in producing this manual.

IT'S NOT ROCKET SCIENCE!

CONTENTS

PHONOLOGICAL AWARENESS — 5

- Word awareness 8
- Syllable Counting 10
- Rhyming 17
- Onset rime 24
- Alliteration 27

SEGMENTATION 1 (IDENTIFICATION OF INITIAL CONSONANT PHONEME) — 31

- Initial Phoneme 's' 32
- Initial Phoneme 'm' 33
- Initial Phoneme 'r' 34
- Initial Phoneme 'l' 35
- Initial Phoneme 'n' 36
- Initial Phoneme 'v' 37
- Initial Phoneme 'f' 38
- Initial Phoneme 'z' 39
- revision (identifying initial Sounds) 40

SEGMENTATION 2 (IDENTIFICATION OF INITIAL CONSONANT PHONEME) — 44

- Final Phoneme 's' 45
- Final Phoneme 'm' 47
- Final Phoneme 'l' 49
- Final Phoneme 'f' 50
- Final Phoneme 'n' 51
- Final Phoneme 'v' 52
- Final Phoneme 'z' 53
- Revision (Identifying Final Sounds) 54

SEGMENTATION 3 (IDENTIFICATION OF INITIAL DIAGRAPHS CONSONANT) — 55

- Initial Consonant Digraph 'sh' as in show 56
- Initial Consonant Digraph Voiced 'th' as in them 57
- Initial Consonant Digraph Voiceless 'th' as in thong 59
- Initial Consonant Digraph 'ch' as in church 61

FINAL SOUNDS — 63

- Final Consonant 'sh' as in show 64
- Final Consonant 'ch' as in church 65
- Final Vowel Sound 'ow' as in cow 67
- Final Letter y (Long vowel sound at end of word) 'y' as in fly 69
- Final Vowel Sound 'oy' as in boy 71
- Final Vowel Sound 'ar' as in car 72
- Final Vowel Sound (Two letter groups, 'o' as in go and 'ow' as in crow) 73

CONTENTS (continued)

INITIAL LONG VOWEL SOUNDS — 74

Initial Long Vowel Sound 'a' as in angel 74
Initial Long Vowel Sound 'e' as in emu 75
Initial Long Vowel Sound 'o' as in oval 76
Initial Long Vowel Sound 'i' as in ice 77

INITIAL SHORT VOWEL SOUNDS — 78

Initial Short Vowel 'a' as in apple 79
Initial Short Vowel "e' as in egg 80
Initial Short Vowel 'i' as Indian 81
Initial Short Vowel 'o' as in orange 82
Initial Short Vowel 'u' as in umbrella 83

IDENTIFICATION OF MEDIAL (MIDDLE) SOUND — 84

Medial Sound 'a' as in cat as in initial 'a' 85
Medial Sound 'e' as in jet as in initial 'e' 86
Medial Sound 'i' as in tin as in initial 'i' 87
Medial Sound 'o' as in cot as in initial 'o' 88
Medial Sound 'u' as in cup as in initial 'u' 89

REMAINING SOUND TO BE TAUGHT — 90

Consonant 'b' 91
Consonant 'k' 92
Consonant 'd' 93
Consonant 'g' 94
Consonant 'j' 95
Consonant 'q' 96
Consonant 'w' 97
Consonant 'x' (cue, k and s) 98
Consonant 'y' 99
Consonant 'p' 101
Consonant 't' 102
Consonant 'k' (as in cat, and also in kitten) 103
Consonant 'th' 104
Consonant 'h' 105

CONTENTS (continued)

BLENDING — 106

- Blending two separate sounds ... 107
- Blending an onset 'c' with a rime, 'at' as with 'c–at' ... 108
- Blending 'at' words, (r–at) ... 109
- Blending 'ot' words, (d–ot) ... 110
- Blending 'it' words, (f–it) ... 111
- Blending 'an' words, (f–an) ... 113
- Blending 'in' words, (f–in) ... 114
- Blending 'on' words, (R–on) ... 115
- Blending 'up' words, (c–up) ... 116

MANIPULATION — 118

- Deletion of the Initial and Second Syllables ... 119
- Deletion of Initial Sound ... 120
- Substitution of Initial Sound ... 122
- Substitution of Final Sound be(d) bet ... 124
- Substitution of Medial Middle Sound b(a)t bit ... 126
- Deletion of the First Sound in an Initial Consonant Blend (c)lean to lean ... 128
- Deletion of the Second Sound in an Initial Consonant Blend b(l)ack to back ... 130
- Deletion of the Final Sound in a Consonant Blend star(t) to star ... 133
- Deletion of the First Sound in a Final Consonant Blend ha(n)d to had ... 134

FOREWORD

Many researchers now believe that the ability to distinguish and isolate the 44 sounds (phonemes) in our english vocabulary is a vital pre-requisite to gaining the skills necessary to read and spell effectively. This process is called phonemic awareness.

PHONEMIC AND PHONOLOGICAL AWARENESS

This is essentially the ability to hear and distinguish differences and similarities in the spoken word. It is purely an auditory process, related to words but occurs in the absence of print, where as phonics is the association of sound and written letter(s)- graphemes. This is a subset of phonological awareness which encorporates auditory analysis skills at a higher level within the word. Phonemic awareness is auditory (sound) awareness at a single sound level, and phonological awareness involves auditory perception at the word and syllable level.

Phonological and phonemic awareness skills are precursors to understanding the alphabetic principle. Children who cannot hear or manipulate the sounds that make up words will have severe difficulty connecting sounds to individual letter symbols and combination of letters *(Adams, 1990)*.

PHONOLOGICAL AWARENESS SKILLS

The basic phonological awareness skills may be divided into the following separate activities:

(a) Word awareness
(b) Syllable Awareness – Syllable Counting
(c) Sub-syllabic Awareness – Onset and Rime
　　　　　　　　　　　　– Rhyming
　　　　　　　　　　　　– Alliteration

PHONEMIC AWARENESS SKILLS

(d) Segmentation 1 (Identifying and Isolating of first sound in a word)
(e) Segmentation 2 (Identifying and isolating final sound in a word)
(f) Segmentation (3) Identifying and isolating first digraph sound in a word eg.
　　/ sh / in shop, / ch / in chip.
　　/g/ Blending
　　/h/ Manipulation, Deletion, Substitution

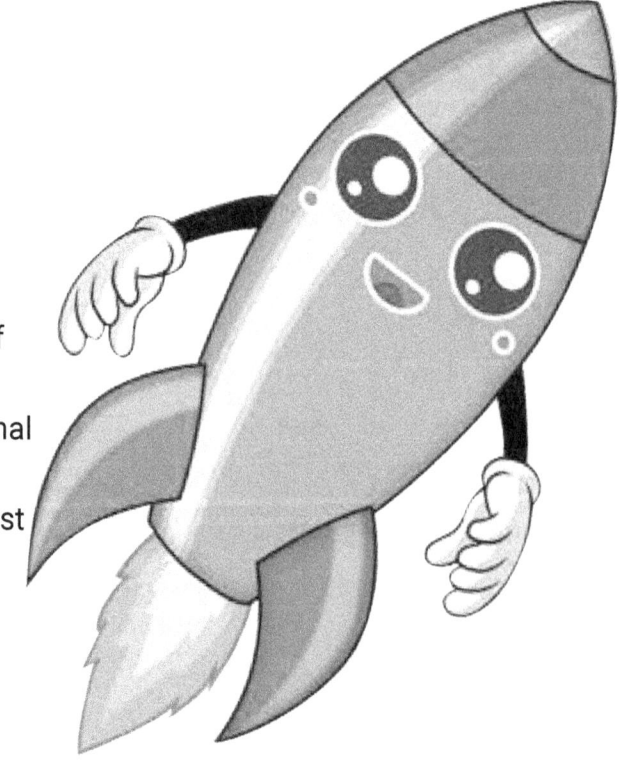

FOREWORD (continued)

This manual is a step-by-step guide designed to assist all beginning readers from pre-school to adults, including ethnic, aboriginal and Torres Strait island groups, and also for students who are learning English as a second language. The focus of the manual is primarily to assist these students to acquire the elementary building blocks on which to scaffold subsequent literacy skills for reading, writing and spelling.

The format and terminology of the instructional lesson plans are designed to guide teachers and other tutors (parents, grandparents teacher aides) in the processes of instruction to aid the acquisition of phonological and phonemic awareness skills in beginning readers.

The letters (graphemes) are included with most lesson plans but letter recognition is not the primary focus at the beginning stage of literacy. attention is drawn to the importance of saying words correctly in order that students can interpret sounds accurately. This is assisted by various hand signs called Cued Articulation. Cued Articulation (CA) is a set of hand cues for teaching the individual sounds in a word. The hand movements are logical, as each hand movement represents one sound and the cue gives clues that indicate how and where the sound is produced.

CA is designed to help all those who find it difficult to remember how to pronounce and/or sequence the sounds of spoken english. The method also helps children who have deficient spelling skills as a result of poor auditory processing skills. (Passy, J) 1990.

Cued Articulation may be referenced in books, a DVD and illustrated cards. Published by Australian Council for Educational Research Ltd. Camberwell, Melbourne, Victoria 3124.

WORD AWARENESS

Word awareness is the knowledge that words have meaning. Students who possess this understanding, can discriminate individual words in spoken or written text. Beginning readers must have this skill before they can extract meaning from what they read.

The sequence of phonological awareness skills starts with understanding spoken words in a sentence.

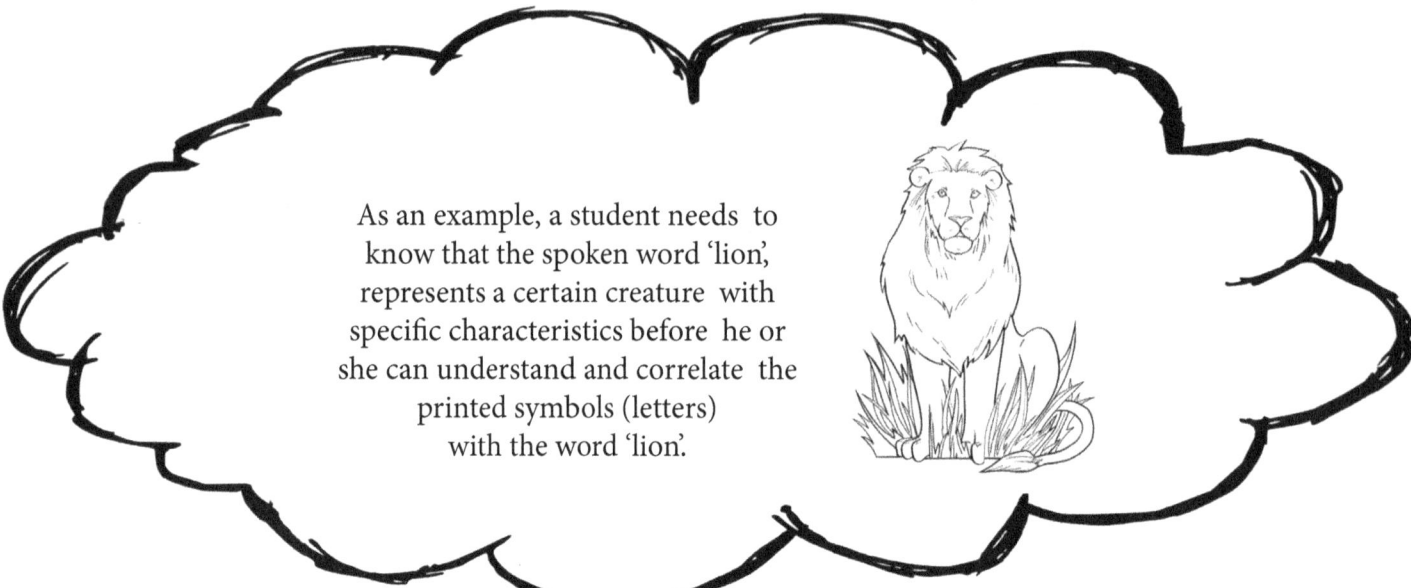

As an example, a student needs to know that the spoken word 'lion', represents a certain creature with specific characteristics before he or she can understand and correlate the printed symbols (letters) with the word 'lion'.

In infants, auditory (hearing) skills develop very early in life and progress to identifying single word meanings, and later to understanding the meaning of a group of words. This skill is progressively refined to the stage of identifying the number of word units within a sentence. As the infant matures to pre-school age this skill is further developed to identifying single sounds within words.

WORD AWARENESS (continued)

SUGGESTED LESSON PLAN

STUDENT OUTCOME

To enable the student to identify separate **word** units by indicating the number of spoken words with the correct number of concrete aids such as buttons, counters or similar tokens.

METHOD

Speech has a direct association with reading and spelling, therefore students need to realise that speech is composed of a number of separate small units called words. in the elementary stages of literacy, students need to be encouraged to attend to word units. This can be achieved by placing a counter (button, coin) for each spoken word in a list of three-four familiar items, e.g. pig, horse cat, bird.

The teacher begins with one word then adds an additional word after each correct response. Repeat process with different list articles until student is proficient in the skill, however with pre-school students, sessions should only be of a few minutes duration and ideally very informal in presentation.

The next step is a progression from listening to a short list of objects to listening to simple two or three word sentences, and placing the correct number of tokens to correspond with the number of words as each sentence is spoken. Gradually increase sentence difficulty.

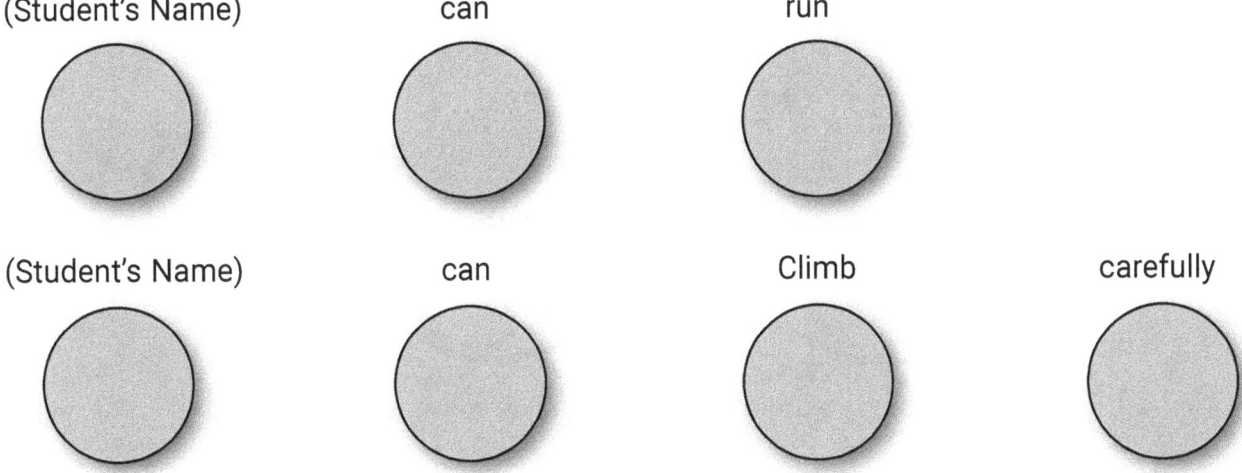

SKILL

Recognising and identifying the correct number of spoken words in a list, or in a sentence, (one-to-one correspondence, that is one token for each spoken word).

EVALUATION

The student is proficient in this skill when individual words can be identified in sentences of varying lengths. This section is usually only applicable for pre- school age children or students learning English as a second language.

SYLLABLE COUNTING

After students understand that sentences are made up of separate word units and these units can be different lengths, the next most important concept for students to understand, is that words are divided into parts or syllables (syllabic awareness). This is a component of phonological awareness.

Syllables are the easiest segments for children to attend to. it can be an individual vowel, or vowels combined with consonant sounds. For example, if we divide the word kang/a/roo into syllables we have three separate parts or three syllables.

Syllables are the foundation blocks of a language, and students who have well-developed phonological skills generally learn to read with more success. These abilities are important in learning about the language, and they provide the foundation for learning the sound print foundation. *(Teacher Vision.com)*

The activities in the following section are designed to encourage students to recognise that words are divided into parts. Each syllable contains a vowel sound as opposed to a vowel letter (the vowel letter 'e' in kite does not have a sound of its own).

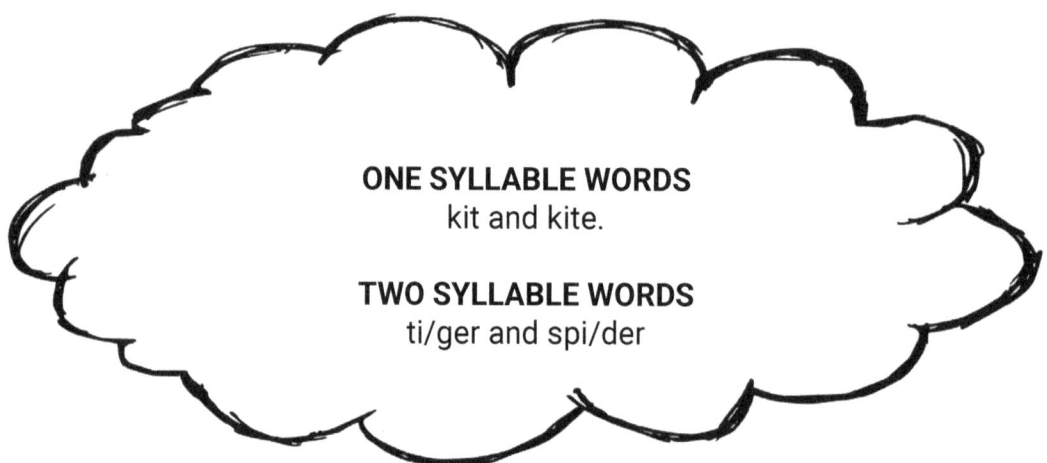

ONE SYLLABLE WORDS
kit and kite.

TWO SYLLABLE WORDS
ti/ger and spi/der

TeacherVision: http://www.teachervision.fen.com/skill-builder/phonics/48601.html#ixzz1fcCAjANe

SYLLABLES

STUDENT OUTCOME
By actively participating in the following exercises a student may recognise that a word may contain only one part, or a number of different parts (syllables).

METHOD
The teacher points to one of the pictures and asks the student to say what the picture represents. The student may say 'cat' and the teacher claps once to demonstrate that the word has one part. The word, 'syllable', may be used, but often beginning readers confuse the words syllables and sounds. As an alternative use the word 'claps' or 'beats'.

ONE CLAP FOR: farm.
TWO CLAPS FOR: farmer

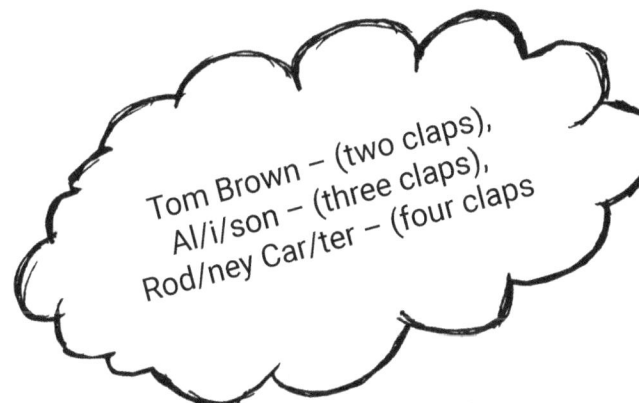

Tom Brown – (two claps),
Al/i/son – (three claps),
Rod/ney Car/ter – (four claps

Compound words are an effective way to promote the concept of syllables, as two distinct and complete words are more meaningful to beginning readers than are parts of words.

For example:
ice-cream, the 'ice' and 'cream' parts are more meaningful than the 'dow' part in window.

Students' and family names are also a good and relevant way for students to understand that words are made up of parts.

SKILL
Identifying that one syllable words require only one clap. Compound words, being two distinct words, need two claps. Multi-syllabic words, need two or more claps. The number of claps therefore corresponding with the same number of syllables.

EVALUATION
Encourage the student to confidently and correctly identify and clap the correct number of parts/syllables, for each picture word.

ONE CLAP FOR: foot.
TWO CLAPS FOR: football.

The next step is to move on to words with three or more syllables. Alternatively the student may place a number of counters (tokens) next to the pictures, to correspond with the number of syllables in the words represented by the pictures.

MONOSYLLABIC WORDS AND PICTURES

ONE SYLLABLE (ONE CLAP)
Pictures to assist syllable counting.

dog   **sun**   **man**   **paint**

play   **ride**   **truck**

train   **horse**   **tree**

car   **race**   **nest**   **house**

  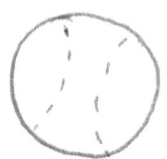

drum   **bike**   **ball**

COMPOUND WORDS

2 SYLLABLES (TWO CLAPS)

Pictures to assist syllable counting.

2 SYLLABLES (TWO CLAPS)

The use of compound words, such as the ones suggested below are meaningful word units and therefore are more easily recognised by students as two distinct units.

star/fish

ice/block

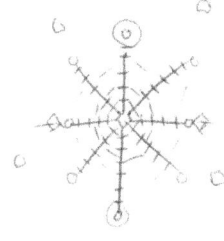
moon/light

play/mates

cow/boy

snow/flake

rain/bow   **fire/wood**   **snow/man**

TWO SYLLABIC WORD COUNTING

flow/er   chick/en   trac/tor

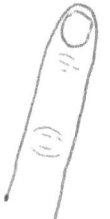  

fing/er   wed/ding   skip/ping

pres/ent   win/dow   tur/key

far/mer   bal/loon   birth/day

MULTIPLE SYLLABIC WORD COUNTING

but/ter/fly

kan/ga/roo

hos/pi/tal

fish/er/man

um/brel/la

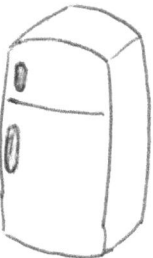
re/frig/er/a/tor

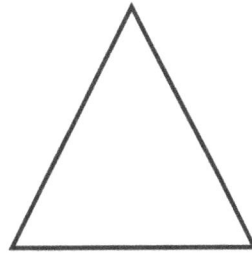
tri/an/gle

MULTIPLE SYLLABIC WORD COUNTING (continued)

tel/e/vi/sion

as/tro/naut

grad/u/ate

car/pen/ter

Aus/tra/lia

tel/e/phone

cat/er/pil/lar

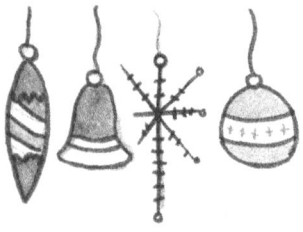

dec/o/ra/tions

com/pu/ter

in/vi/ta/tion

RHYMING

Many researchers suggest that rhyming is one of the key skills of phonological awareness that precedes the more specific skill of phonemic awareness. Rhyming and nursery rhymes should ideally be introduced as early as possible, before pre-school and formal education.

A crucial stage in phonological awareness development is evident when children/students can attend to the structure of a word, whereby words can be classified according to rime, that is the final or end sound.

Rhyming activities and nursery rhymes should therefore form part of both formal and informal teaching practices.

IDENTIFYING PATTERNS

Words contain many patterns, and emergent readers often discover patterns when introduced to nursery rhymes and rhyming word families. rhymes expose pre and beginning readers to new words, thus increasing their vocabulary, which is an important component of comprehension.

Student(s) complete(s) the sentence with a rhyming word after teacher says the first part. nonsense words should be accepted. They can add humour!

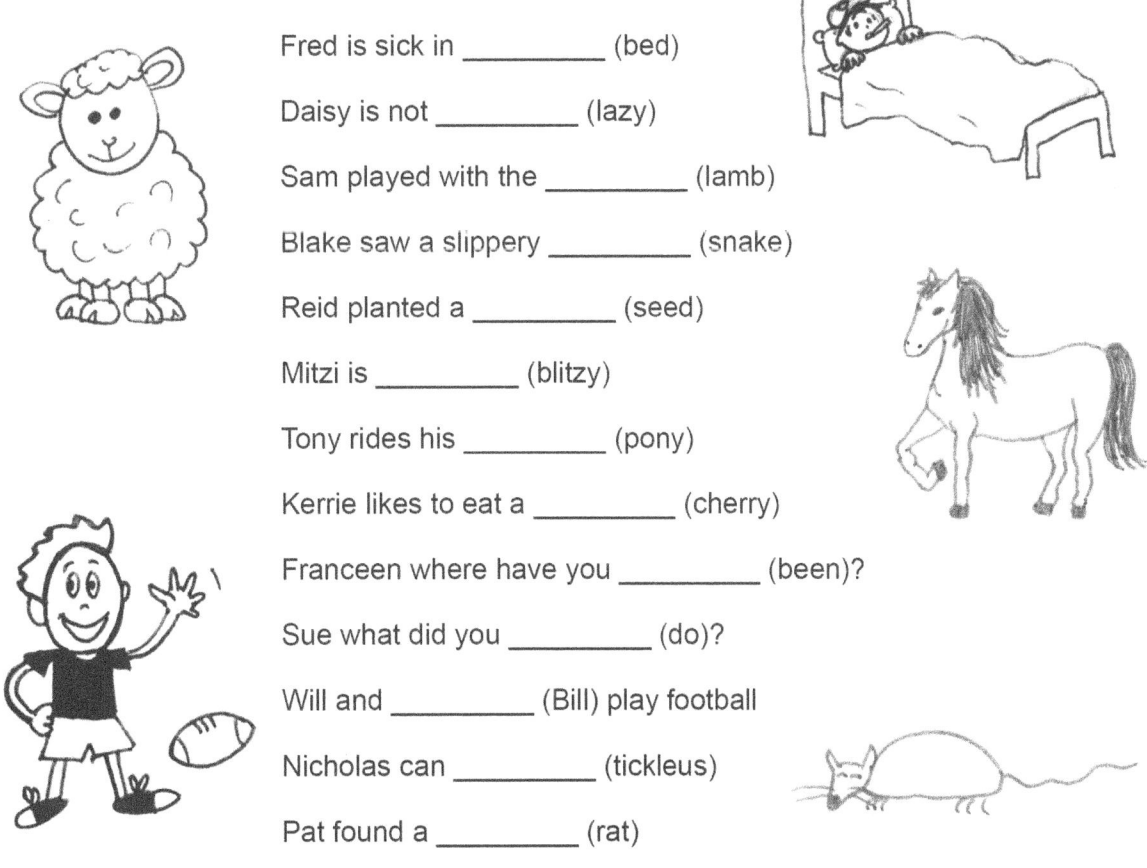

Fred is sick in _____ (bed)

Daisy is not _____ (lazy)

Sam played with the _____ (lamb)

Blake saw a slippery _____ (snake)

Reid planted a _____ (seed)

Mitzi is _____ (blitzy)

Tony rides his _____ (pony)

Kerrie likes to eat a _____ (cherry)

Franceen where have you _____ (been)?

Sue what did you _____ (do)?

Will and _____ (Bill) play football

Nicholas can _____ (tickleus)

Pat found a _____ (rat)

Did you see Dave _____ (wave)?

Read more: What Are the Benefits of Rhyming in Literacy? | eHow.com
http://www.ehow.com/info_10001327_benefits-rhyming-literacy.html#ixzz1fcyxTRPl

RHYMING

SUGGESTED ACTIVITIES

Recite nursery rhymes and encourage the child to say the rhymes with you as the words become more familiar to the child. The use of books with colourful illustrations adds to the enjoyment. The more formal aspects of rhyming may be introduced with the following picture activities found on page 13, 14, 15 and 16.

PICTURES FOR RHYMING PAIRS (OR THREES)

The teacher shows two/three pictures and says what they represent. The child/student is then asked, 'Do these words sound nearly the same'?

If the student has difficult with this task say the words slowly, emphasising the rime (the last part of each word.) The student may suggest a different action for rhyming and non-rhyming words, such as, thumbs up for rhymes. Thumbs down for non-rhyming words. The lesson plan suggested on the following page may be used.

When the student confidently demonstrates the previous skills he/she may suggest words that rhyme without the picture cues. The teacher says word(s) e.g. book-look, child adds took (or similar rhyming word), dad-lad, child adds sad.

The following are just a few examples where the teacher gives the initial words and the student supplies an additional one or two words;

mum-some, _____

girl-curl, _____

boy-toy, _____

play-way, _____

car-far, _____

tree-see, _____

fun-won, _____

ride-side, _____

bed-fed, _____

book-look, _____

soap-rope, _____

RHYMING (continued)

Words and nonsense words with a greater number of phonemes (sounds) may be used if appropriate i.e. if the student can easily identify smaller rhyming words as those listed above.

With the following words the student may make the thumbs up sign for rhyming words and thumbs down for non-rhyming words and a clap for a rhyming nonsense (non-dictionary) words. Some researchers suggest that the use of nonsense words assists in the learning of a particular skill. At this stage it is the rhyming skill of recognising unknown words that rhyme, that is the rhyming section of each word. Students usually enjoy the different 'funny' sounds of these words and the rhyming concept is reinforced.

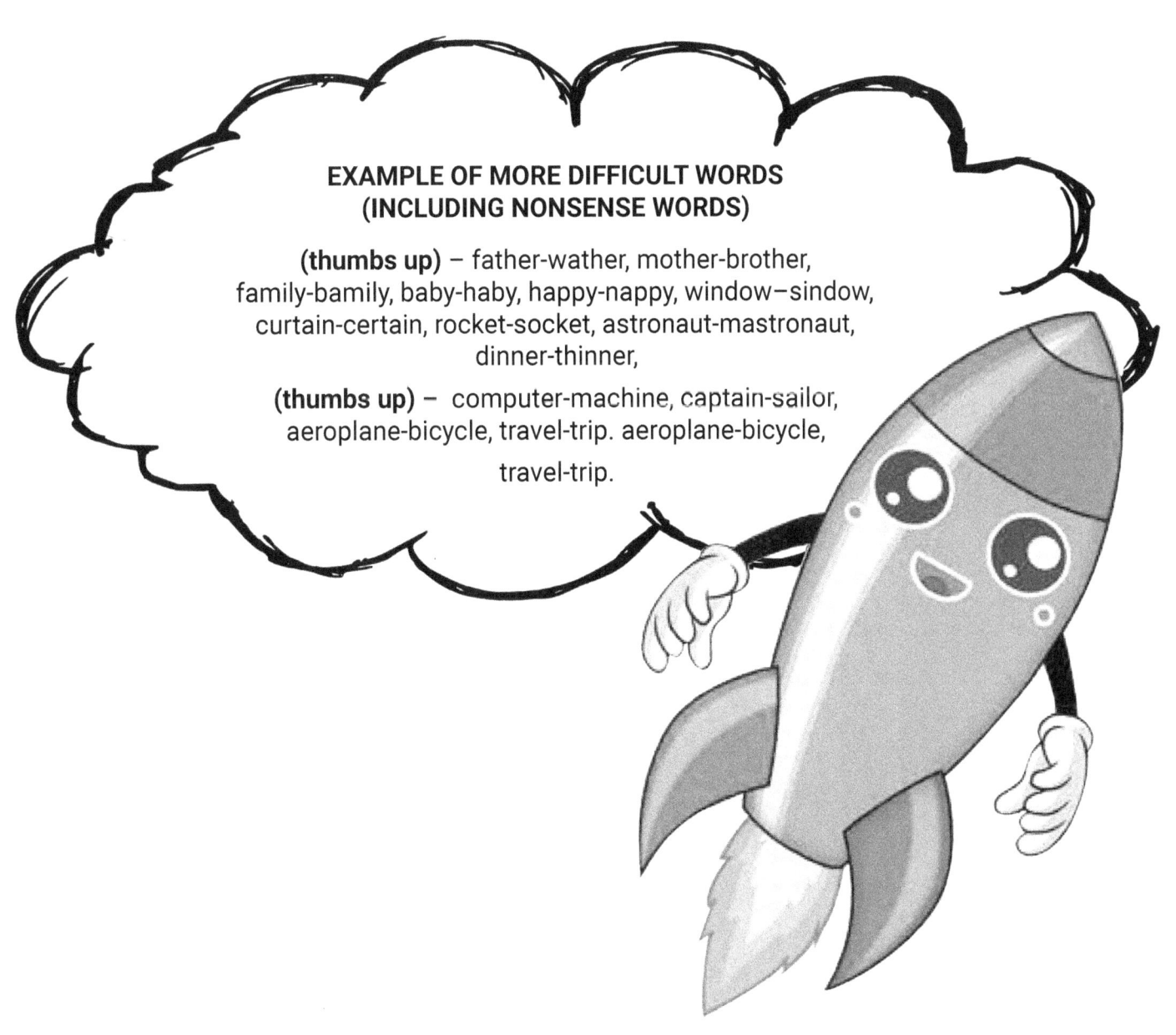

EXAMPLE OF MORE DIFFICULT WORDS (INCLUDING NONSENSE WORDS)

(**thumbs up**) – father-wather, mother-brother, family-bamily, baby-haby, happy-nappy, window–sindow, curtain-certain, rocket-socket, astronaut-mastronaut, dinner-thinner,

(**thumbs up**) – computer-machine, captain-sailor, aeroplane-bicycle, travel-trip. aeroplane-bicycle, travel-trip.

SYLLABLES

STUDENT OUTCOME
The student identifies the rhyming section of a word, and then pairs it with a matching rhyming word picture.

METHOD
Firstly the teacher may choose two pictures and says the words represented by the pictures. The student is then asked if these two words sound almost the same at the end. Repeat the process a number of times. When the student demonstrates an understanding of this task, move to more difficult ones such as:

(a) Choose the two rhyming pictures from three pictures.

(b) Choose two/three rhyming pictures from a small group of pictures.

(c) Put all the pictures into their rhyming groups.

SKILL
Matching, rhyming words with appropriate rhyming pictures.

EVALUATION
Students are competent in these rhyming tasks when they demonstrate the ability to identify word endings that sound alike, that is, they rhyme.

RHYMING PICTURES

bat   mat   cat   mug   bug   rug   boy   toy   joy

*Cut and sort into family groups, e.g. 'at' family, 'ug' family, etc.
Pictures may be pasted and colored in family groups, at a later time.*
(Remember to check that the student knows the object or activity depicted by the illustration)

RHYMING PICTURES (continued)

car star jar tree sea bee curl girl pearl dad sad bad

RHYMING PICTURES (continued)

cap tap map dog log jog ten pen hen

ONSET RHYME/RIME

Onset rime has been shown to be one of the most effective ways of improving phonological awareness according to *(Adams, 1990)*.

Onset and rime are phonological (sound) units that make up a syllable. a syllable can be separated into two distinct parts, the initial consonant and then the vowel, plus any other consonants. in the words paint and saint 'p' and 's' are the onsets and 'aint' forms the rime section. Rime is similar to rhyme in that they each form a rhyming pattern, however the word rime shows that the spelling pattern is consistent, whereas in rhyme the spelling may change, but the sound pattern at the end of the word remains the same, for example the words blue and flew rhyme but the spelling changes, that is, the spelling is not a consistent pattern.

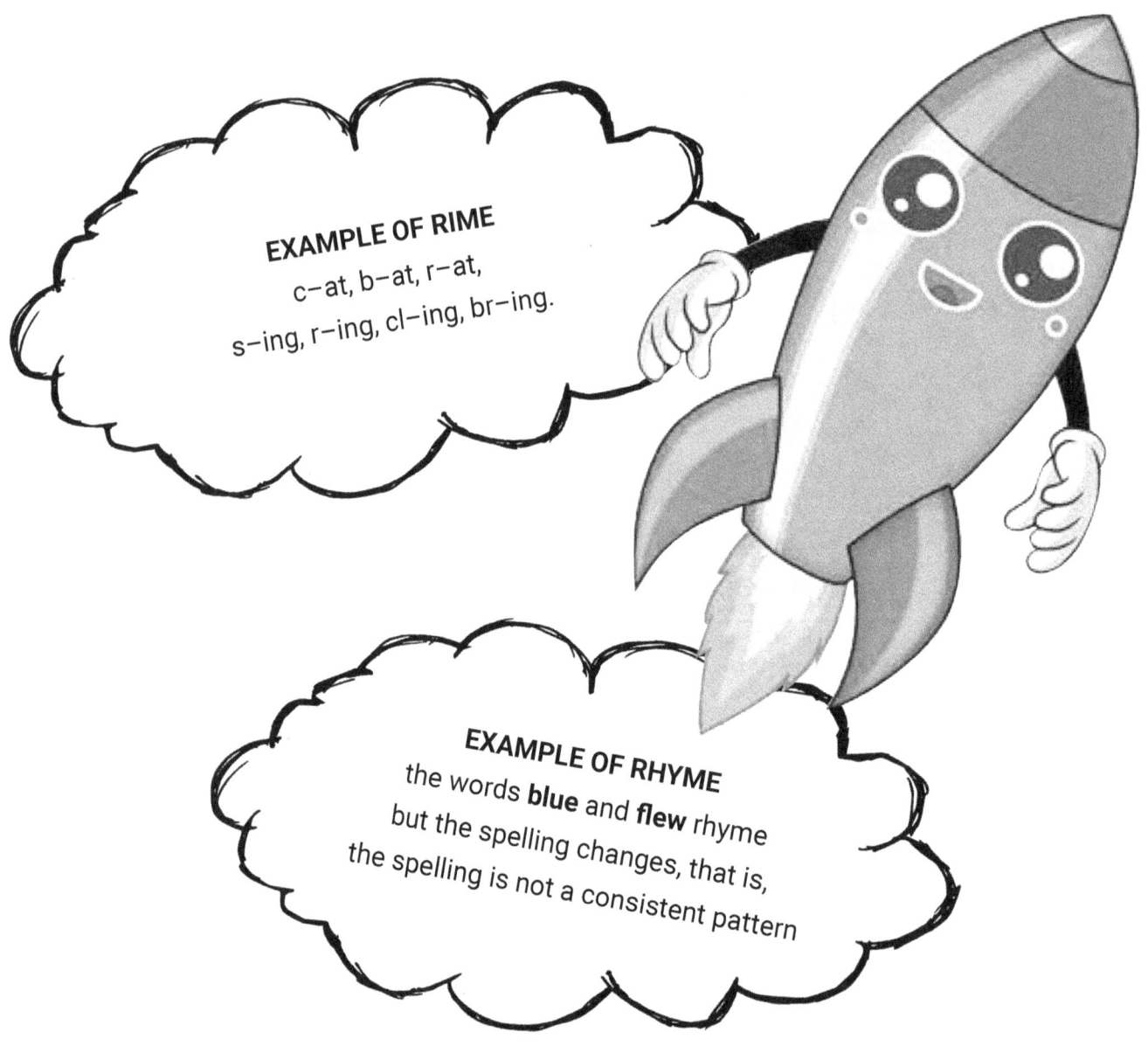

EXAMPLE OF RIME
c–at, b–at, r–at,
s–ing, r–ing, cl–ing, br–ing.

EXAMPLE OF RHYME
the words **blue** and **flew** rhyme but the spelling changes, that is, the spelling is not a consistent pattern

---

Adams, M. (1990) *Beginning to read: Thinking and Learning about Print*. Cambridge. MA: MIT Press

ONSET AND RIME (continued)

LESSON OUTCOME
The student is encouraged to recognise that a monosyllabic (one syllable) word has two parts, (as distinct from syllables) the onset and the rime. From a given onset the student gives the rime to complete the word.

METHOD
Explain to the student that you are going to say some words slowly and there will be two parts. The teacher demonstrates by pointing to the picture of the cat on the following page and says, 'The word cat, is broken into two parts 'c' (the onset) and 'at' (the rime).

Now ask the student 'How many parts did you hear?'.

The student should recognise both parts and answer, 'Two'.

Using the additional pictures on the page the teacher may then say the onset and request the student to supply a rime.

Tokens may be used to illustrate the two parts of the word. The teacher may place a token for the onset and the student places a token for the rime.

The next step may be to practise the same procedure without the aid of a picture. The teacher articulates a word beginning with 'm' the student replies with 'at', or any number of rimes such as: 'ake', 'en', 'ix', 'ud', 'ap', 'iss'. The onset letter is also varied to make other monosyllabic words.

SKILLS
Identifying the rime section of a word with the aid of pictures and then from oral stimulus only, that is, the spoken word.

EVALUATION
The student demonstrates the ability to supply the rime section of a word with and without visual stimulus (pictures).

PICTURES FOR ONSET RIME ACTIVITIES

cat mat bat rug mug bug ten hen men hot pot dot

ALLITERATION

Alliteration is the use of the same initial sound in words, with this sound being repeated a number of times in prose or in verse.

It is the sound not the letter that is important, as it is the sound that makes the repetitive pattern. This does not mean that the same initial letter makes the alliteration pattern as in 'car' and 'cent'. However the same sound pattern can be represented by different letters as in 'car' and 'kids and the alliteration pattern is sustained.

> Dr. Pam Schiller suggests that alliteration is an important literacy concept for children to learn. It precedes a child's ability to make sound/symbol relationships,... and it is important that they are able to tell you the sound they hear, and less important that they can identify the letter that makes the sound.

Alliteration is a fun way for young children to experience phonemic (sound) awareness and at the same time develop concentration and memory skills. Alliteration is also an effective way to promote auditory discrimination (the ability to identify particular sounds in words.) This particular skill being the recognition of a repetitive initial sound).

Schiller, P. www.pamschiller.com
http://kimboed.com/activitytips0206.aspx

ALLITERATION (continued)

STUDENT OUTCOME

The outcome for these activities is primarily that the student enjoys saying sentences in the form of verse that develops a specific sound pattern of repetition and beat. As auditory discrimination develops students may be able to identify target sounds in each verse.

METHOD

As a method of introduction the teacher may ask questions relating to student's knowledge of any of the creatures mentioned in the rhymes, (on the following pages). tell the student that you are going to tell him/her about a frog in a little story called verse or poetry.

Discuss with the student what was different about that type of story. The answer may be that it was short and quick and you can clap as you say it, or there were lots of 'f' or 's' sounds. Repeat the rhyme (s) two or three times or until the student begins to lose interest, and this may only be a few minutes.

SKILLS

Recognising that verse has a rhythm or beat that is different from prose, and that it also has a particular repetitive sound.

EVALUATION

The measure of assessment for this skill may be the ability of the student to correctly repeat, part or all of a rhyme, the degree of enjoyment gained and finally the recognition of a common or repeating sound. As students' literacy skills progress they will understand that the same letter does not always make the same sound and vice versa, for example 'c' in car and 'c' in cent, same letter different sound, but 's' in sent and also in cent, has the same sound, but different letters.

ALLITERATION (continued)

PRACTICE SAYING THESE VERSES WITH YOUR STUDENT

Freddie Frog flops and flips
Flopping here and flipping there
Flipping, flopping every Friday
Freddie is a flipping, flopping frog.

Gertie Goat, Gertie Goat
Greedily grazing
On green grass.
Gobbling, gobbling
Grapes and gooseberries
greedy, greedy
gertie goat.

Gertie Goat, Gertie Goat
Greedily grazing
On green grass.
Gobbling, gobbling
Grapes and gooseberries
greedy, greedy
gertie goat.

Porky, porky Percy Pig
Prancing, prancing in the puddles
Playfully playing in the puddles
Porky, porky Percy Pig.

Annie Ant, Annie Ant,
Artistic, Annie Ant,
She's an acrobat and an artist
She has ability and a agility
Amazing amazing Annie Ant.

The above ditties may be enlarged and student(s) may then wish to cut, paste and colour them in their own little booklets. Such an activity will assist in memorizing the verses and may assist in establishing the recognition of the alliteration principle.

Please note the letter 'a' has various sounds, for example ant, ability and artist all have a different initial sound.

IDENTIFICATION OF INITIAL PHONEME (Sound)

In oral language – that is when we speak, sounds are quickly blended together to make a word. When we say the word 'sun' we are blending the three sounds together s-u-n to make the word 'sun'.

When students begin to match sounds to letters – that is when spelling – they need to be able to take words apart by identifying each sound. This process is called segmentation.

The first segmentation task is the identification of the initial sound in a spoken word.

The second task is that of identifying the final sound. The third and final segmentation skill is to identify the medial sound in a monosyllabic word, for example, the 'a' sound in cat. Students usually find this task quite difficult as the short vowel sounds (a, e, i, o, u) are blended with the initial and final consonants making the isolation task more difficult than segmenting the initial or final sound.

Letter symbols have been included with each worksheet, but it is at the teacher's discretion when the optimum time may be for the introduction of written symbols (graphemes).

IDENTIFICATION OF INITIAL PHONEME

STUDENT OUTCOME

The student is encouraged to isolate and identify the initial sound in a word beginning with a consonant that has a continuous sound (called a continuant consonant).

This is the first stage of segmentation, and the choice of a continuant consonant assists the initial isolation of the target sound. The use of pictures aids the short-term memory retention of the target word.

METHOD

The tutor chooses from one of the following continuant (long or extended sounding) consonants s, m, r, l, f, n, v, z. These may be taught in any order. The 's' sound is a good choice for developing this student outcome. The remaining listed consonants may be taught using this method.

The teacher points to one of the pictures (on the following page) and articulates the word slowly, e.g. sss u n.

The cued hand sign may also be demonstrated. The student is now encouraged to isolate and say the initial sound as he/she also demonstrates the cued hand sign. The teacher may ask 'What sound did you hear at the beginning when I started to say the word ssss-u-n?'

Encourage the student to watch your changing lips and mouth shape as you say the complete word. Repeat with other 's' words.

SKILLS

Identifying the initial consonant sound in a number of words aided by visual stimuli (pictures) and tactile stimuli (cued hand signs).

EVALUATION

After saying all picture words and demonstrating an understanding of the initial sound in these words, show a picture of a word beginning with a different sound and ask the student if this picture begins with the 's' sound.

If the answer is 'no', proceed to next sound, that is, one of the sustaining continuant listed in the Method section of this lesson or leave the new sound until the next session. remember, at this stage the focus is on the target phoneme, ('s' for this session) not the letter. However, as the sessions continue many students will develop an association with letter sound relationships and the appropriate letter symbols may be placed/pasted and/or written next to the pictures.

Use the above format for teaching the auditory identification of the remaining continuant consonants, m, r, l, n, v, f, z in the initial position of spoken words.

Illustrations of these hand signs or cues for these initial consonants, may be found in Jane Passy's books, DVD and illustrated cards.

PICTURES FOR THE INITIAL CONSONANT "s"

sun soup soap sip sand soda sit six sleep

Although the primary focus is sound identification, each page may be photocopied and the sound pasted next to a picture.

| s | s | s | s | s | s | s | s | s |

PICTURES FOR THE INITIAL CONSONANT "m"

monkey mum moon mouse mountain man mail mat map

PICTURES FOR THE INITIAL CONSONANT "r"

rabbit   rainbow   robot   rod   rat   rake   ring   rope   rose

PICTURES FOR THE INITIAL CONSONANT "l"

lion   lips   lollypop   lamb   leaf   lid   lady   leg   lamp

PICTURES FOR THE INITIAL CONSONANT "n"

nest   net   nine   nose   night   neck   necklace   numbers   nut

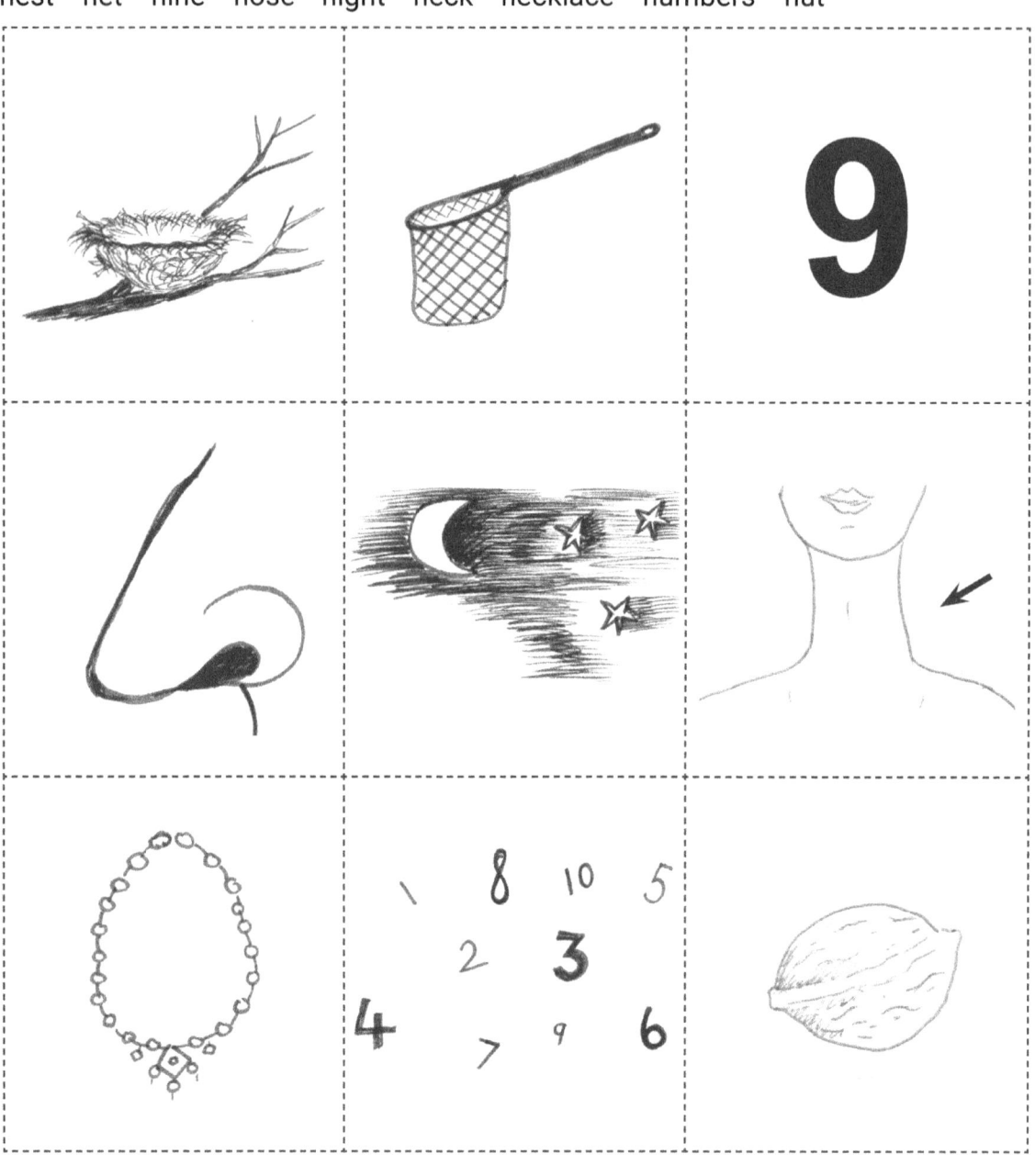

PICTURES FOR THE INITIAL CONSONANT "v"

van vase violin veil vegetables vulture vest violet volcano

v	v	v	v	v	v	v	v	v

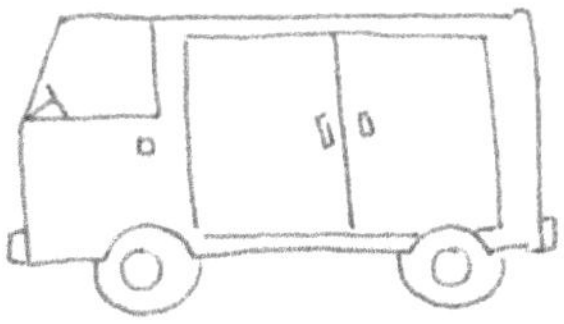

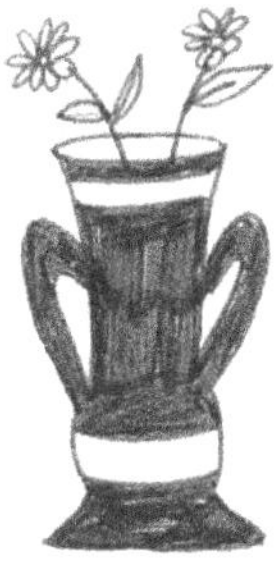

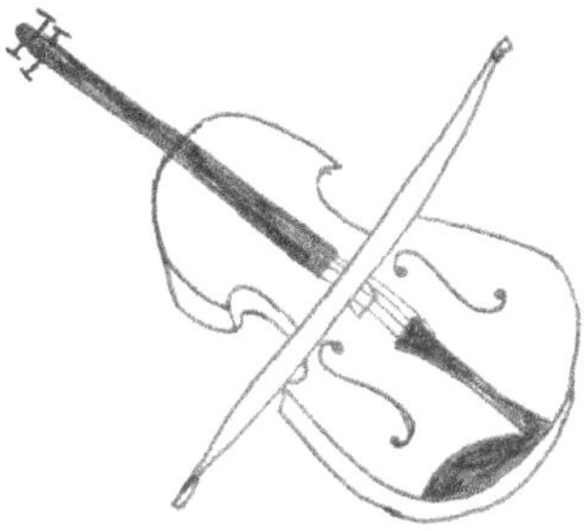

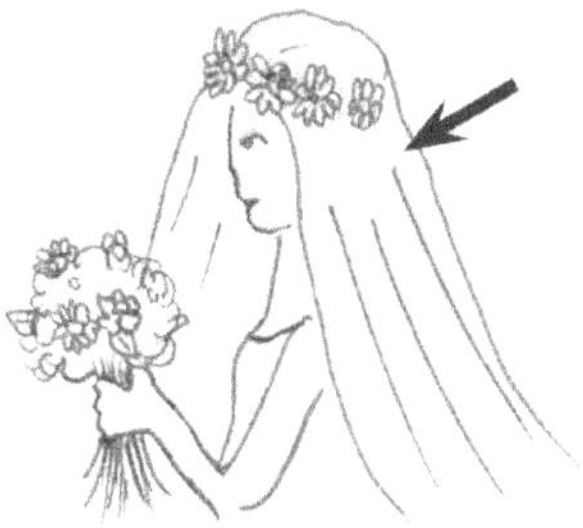

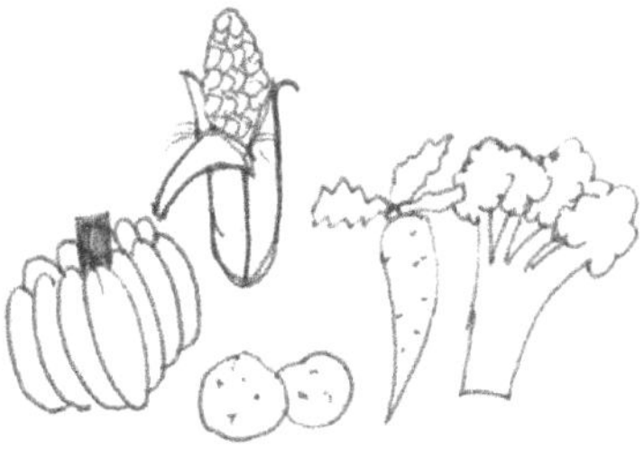

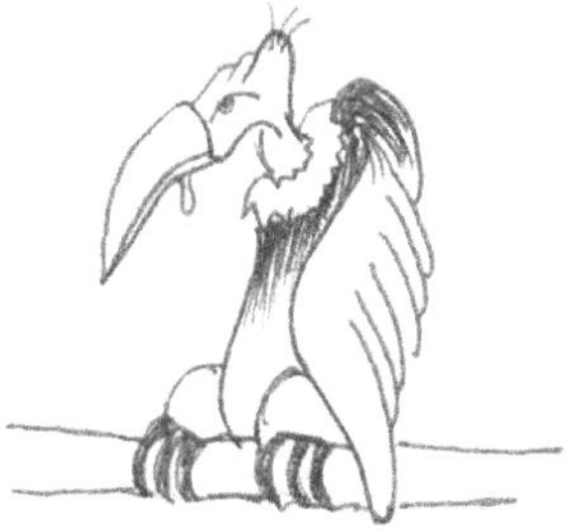

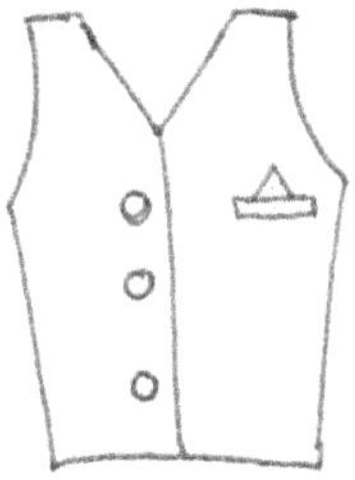

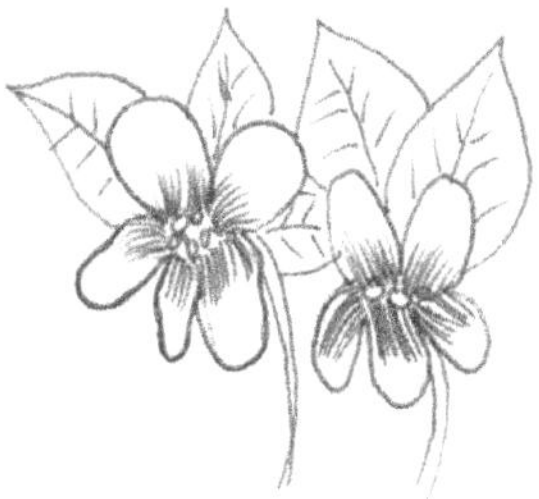

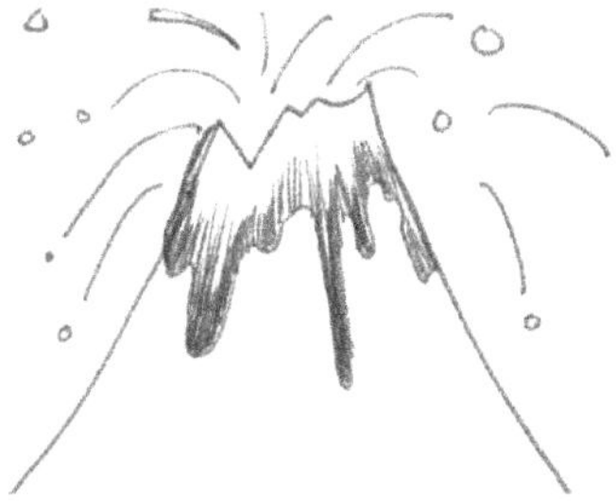

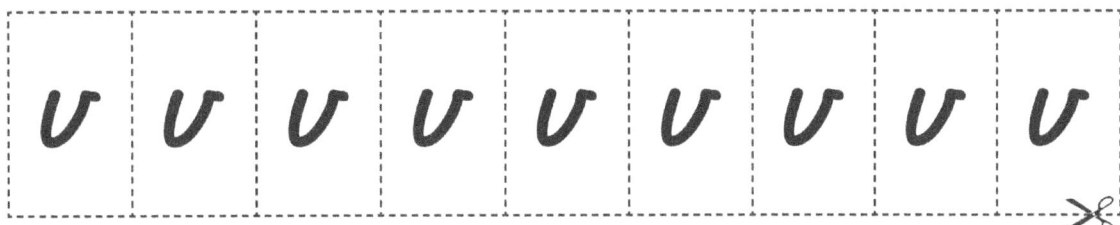

PICTURES FOR THE INITIAL CONSONANT "f"

football fox fence face four five fish footprints fan

PICTURES FOR THE INITIAL CONSONANT "z"

zebra zig-zag zip zoo zoom zero

REVISION OF INITIAL CONSONANTS

The following exercise may be undertaken as a form of evaluation to determine a student's ability to identify and associate an initial sound with a picture and the spoken word. The student may be requested to colour (tick, circle, stick a dot beside or point to) the pictures with the beginning sound 's'.

Choose another sound and repeat the process with a different activity to identify these particular pictures/words. It may be 'm'. Again it is not necessary to use the corresponding letters for the pictures but they may be used if the teacher deems this beneficial.

Pictures for the revision of initial sounds, s, m, r, l, n, v, z may be found on the following three pages.

PICTURES FOR THE INITIAL SOUNDS (Revision)

rocket fish leaf zebra van snake moon nest rabbit

r f l ʒ v s m n r

PICTURES FOR THE INITIAL SOUNDS (continued)

monkey   rainbow   leopard   vase   lion   five   zip   soap   volcano

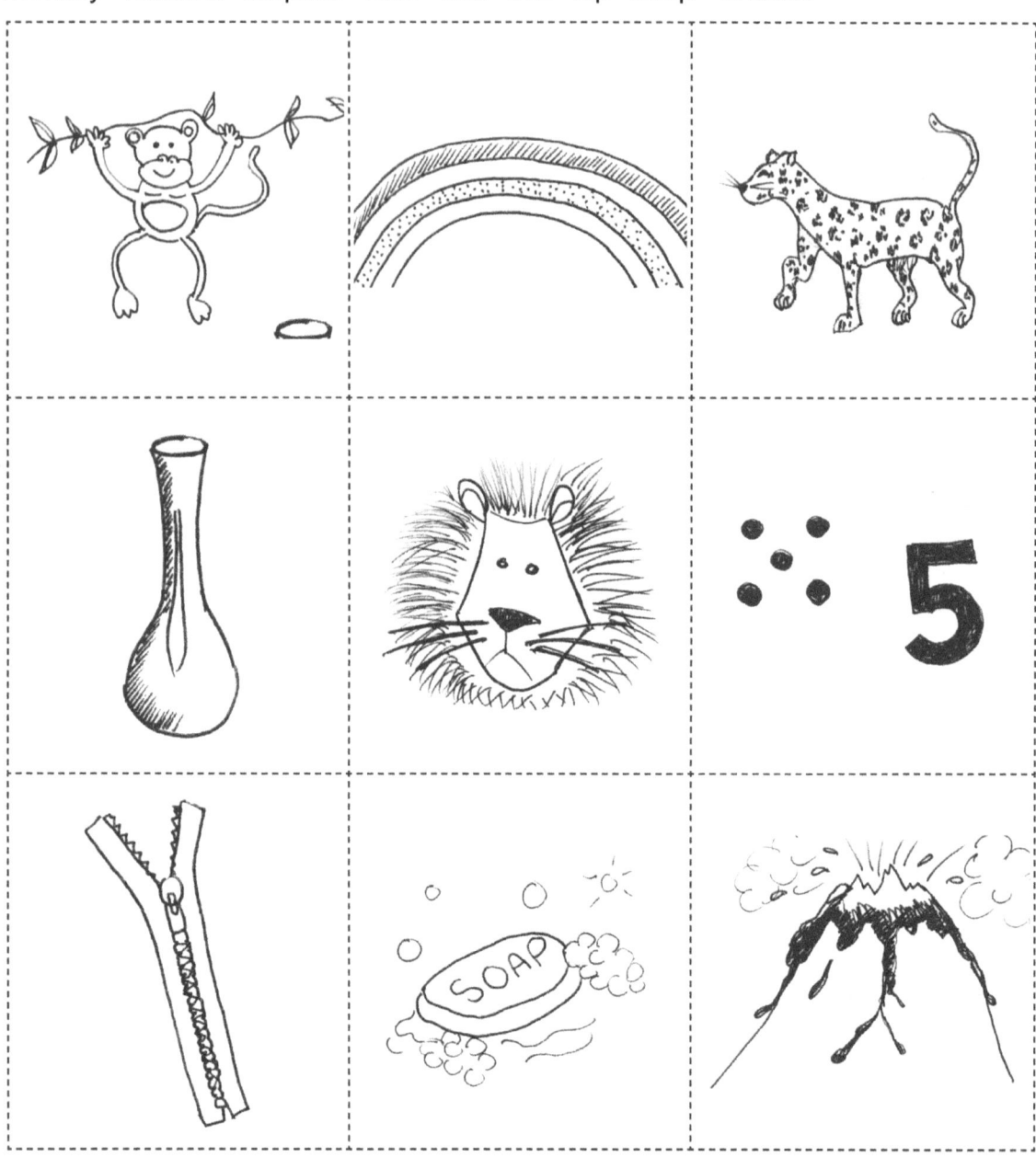

| m | r | l | v | l | f | 3 | s | v |

PICTURES FOR THE INITIAL SOUNDS (continued)

nut lollypop violin rabbit monkey face zigzag football sock

| n | l | v | r | m | f | ʒ | f | s |

IDENTIFICATION OF FINAL PHONEME

The focus for this section is on the identification of the final consonant in each spoken word. As with the first segmentation exercises, these consonants, are also the ones most easily identified because the sound can be extended and emphasised.

STUDENT OUTCOME
the student is encouraged to isolate and identify the initial sound in a word beginning with a consonant that has a continuous sound (called a continuant consonant).

METHOD

Explain to the student that you are going to say a word slowly, but this time i would like you to listen and watch the speech organs (mouth, lips, teeth, tongue) in order to tell me the last sound that you hear. This method may be used to teach other final consonant sounds listed in this section (m, l, f, n, v, z).

Say with exaggerated lip movements k-i-ssss. ask student to identify the last sound.

Practise the skill with words such as cross, boss, kiss, glass, class, brass, mouse, house, purse.

Where possible, point to a picture to correspond with the spoken word.

Note at this stage the focus is purely on the last sound. When the final letter is 'e' as in the spelling of face and space, the letter 'e' is a 'silent' letter but the final sound is still 's'.

Repeat words (plus any additional ones you can add). Encourage student to cue the 's' sound as each word is spoken.

SKILLS

Identification of final phoneme.

EVALUATION

When the student correctly cues the final 's' sound, the teacher may randomly add words with a different final sound. Instruct student to only cue when the final sound is 's' or 'ss' spelling. Face, fence, bless, boss, cross, place.

The 'ce' blocks may be used at the teacher's discretion. The words may be partly written by the teacher and the student pastes the final sounds.

FURTHER EVALUATION TASKS

Words with the 's' sound in the initial or final position are clearly spoken and the student cues the sound at the appropriate time.

SKILL

Identification of final and initial phoneme.

SUGGESTED WORDS AND PICTURES FOR FOR THE FINAL "s" SOUND

face kiss floss bus boss space fence cross race

(Remember do not place 's' next to words such as space, fence, race.)

WORDS AND PICTURES FOR FINAL PHONEME "s"

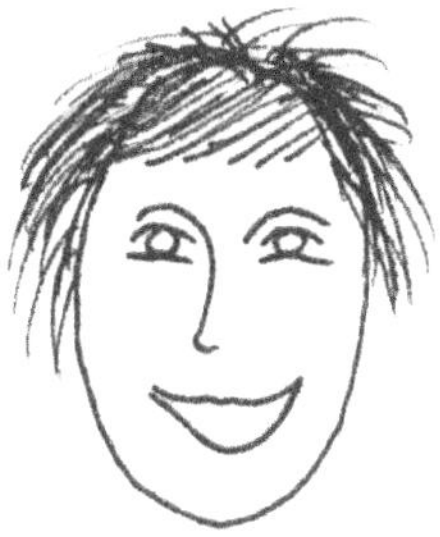
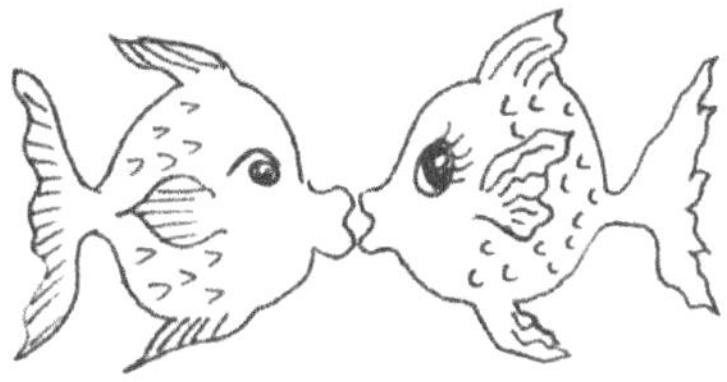
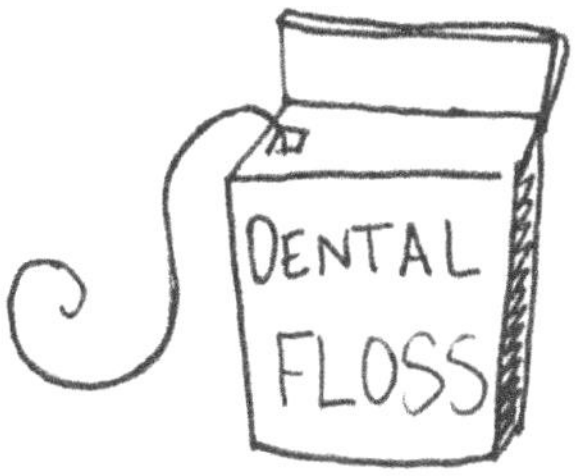

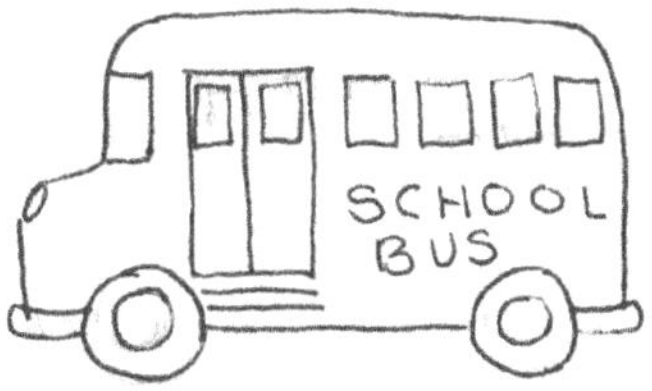

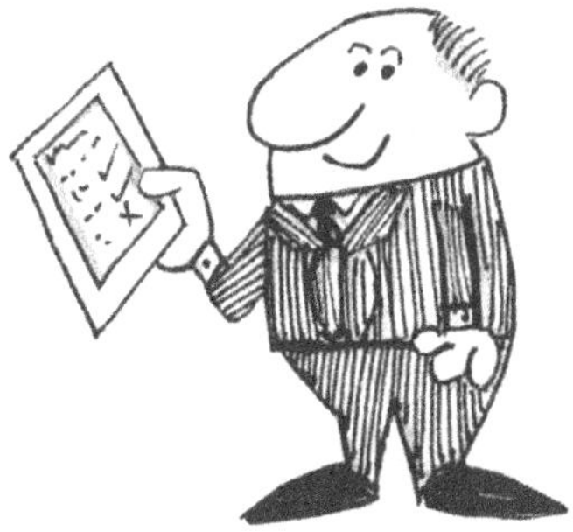
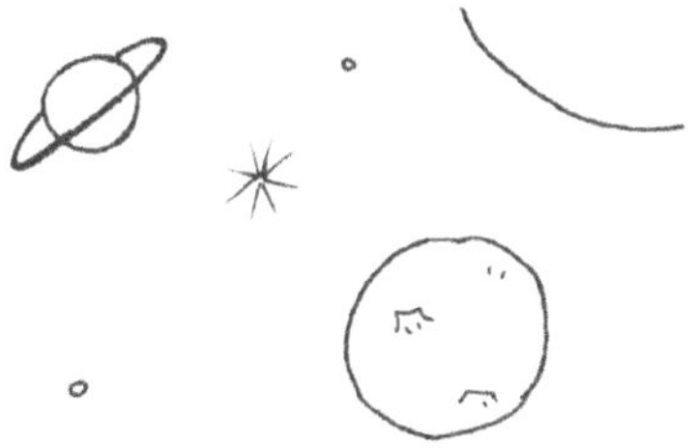
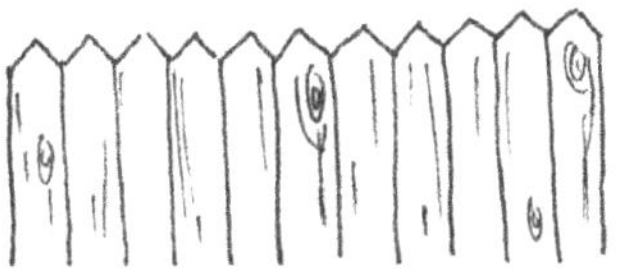
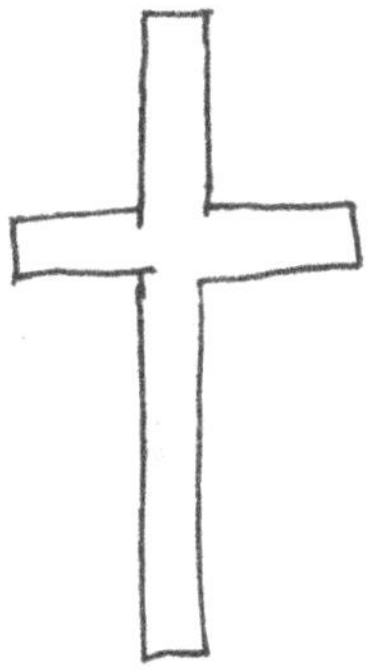
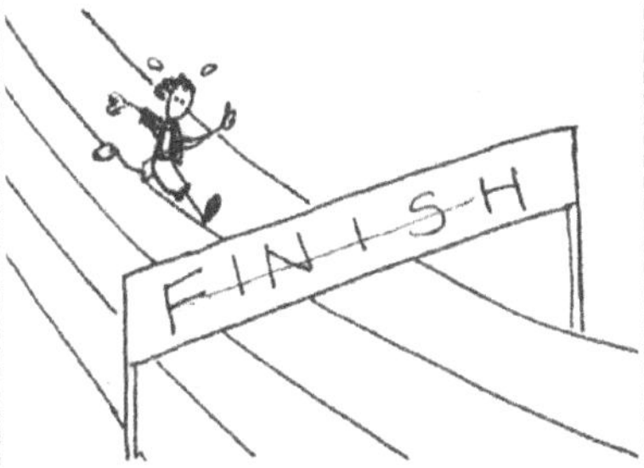

The blocks below may be cut out and placed next to pictures with final s spelling e.g. cross, boss, floss, bus.

ce	ss	ss	s	ss	ce	ce	ss	ce

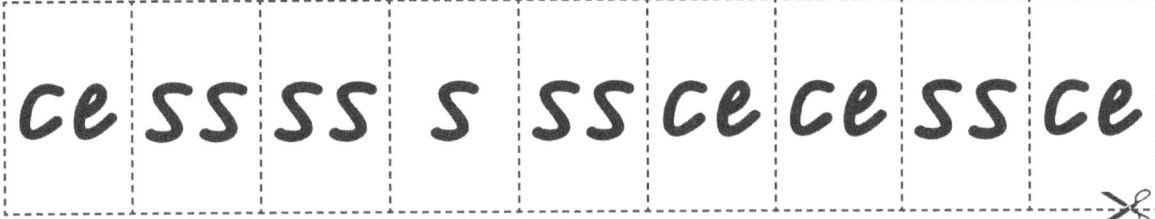

SUGGESTED WORDS AND PICTURES FOR THE FINAL CONSONANT SOUND

The following final consonants (with the exception of 'r') may be taught using the same lesson plans as previously outlined in the Student outcome, Method and evaluation. Suggested order for teaching the following final consonants: m, l. f, n, v, z. In the English language it is not common to have a 'pure' 'r' sound in the final position. Therefore, the 'r' sound has not been included in this section. The initial sound 'r' in rat is not the same as the final 'r' in river.

SKILL

Identifying the final consonant in a number of words with visual stimuli (pictures) and also in spoken words and non-dictionary or nonsense words.

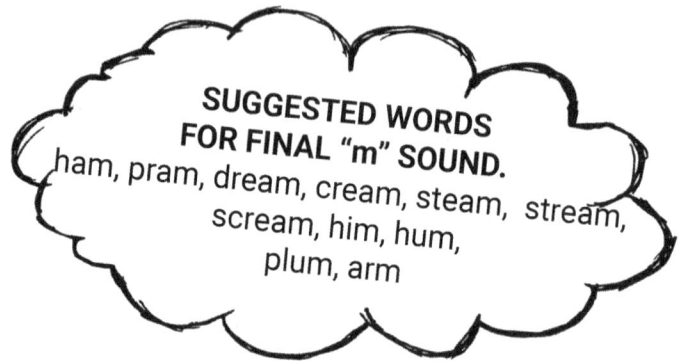

SUGGESTED WORDS FOR FINAL "m" SOUND.
ham, pram, dream, cream, steam, stream, scream, him, hum, plum, arm

ADDITIONAL EVALUATION

The tutor may now point to one of the pictures and explain to the student that she/he is going to say the first part of the word for example p r a.... and the student is to add the final 'm' sound followed by the completed word 'pram'.

The hand cue for 'm' may also be used as the sound is made, or if necessary, the tutor may cue **before** the sound is articulated. This may assist a more fluent blending and recognition of the target word pram.

Some researchers believe pseudo-words or non-dictionary words are a useful evaluation tool. I will therefore, suggest some non-words that you may like to try in order to test the student's ability to identify the target sound (final 'm') with words such as, flum, sprum, brum, crim, schom, plarm, bleem, scrom, praylim etc. This enables a more accurate assessment of the principle skill, as there would have been no previous exposure to these words.

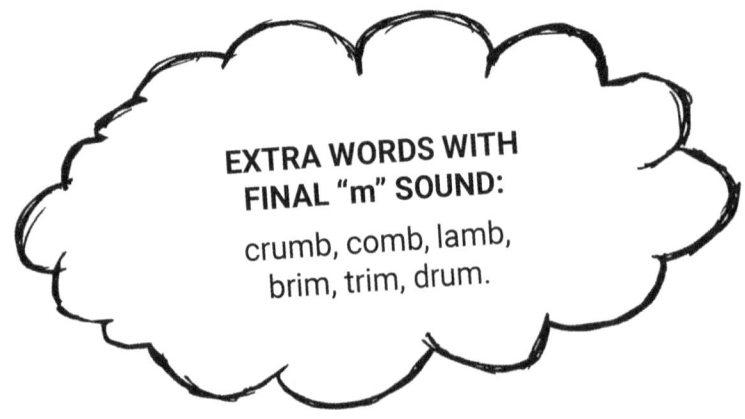

EXTRA WORDS WITH FINAL "m" SOUND:
crumb, comb, lamb, brim, trim, drum.

The usefulness of pseudowords is illustrated by Keith Stanovich (2000) who suggests that pseudo-words can clearly define the better, from the poorer readers at all levels. Furthermore, Stanovich cites the application of phonic rules to the effectiveness of decoding written words.

REFERENCES:
Stanovich, k.e. (2000) *Progress in Understanding Reading*. New York, NY: Guilford.

SUGGESTED WORDS AND PICTURES FOR FOR THE FINAL "m" SOUND

ham worm plum pram arm drum lamb comb sum

The 'm' blocks below may be cut and placed next to pictures with final 'm' spelling, for example, ham, cream, plum, pram, drum, arm.

(The teacher may explain that 'comb' and 'lamb' have a letter 'b' that doesn't have a sound.)

CONSONANTS IN THE FINAL POSITION

The remaining consonants in the final position, m, l, f, n, v, z may be taught according to the previously stated plan for Student outcomes, Method and Evaluation, but substituting the previously taught sound with each new sound as it is introduced.

The phoneme 'r' in the final position is influenced by the preceding vowel, and therefore, has a number of different sounds.

The 'r' at the end of 'roar' is not pronounced in the same way as the initial 'r' in roar or rabbit. The final 'r' in 'roar' combines with the preceding vowels to make the 'oar' sound.

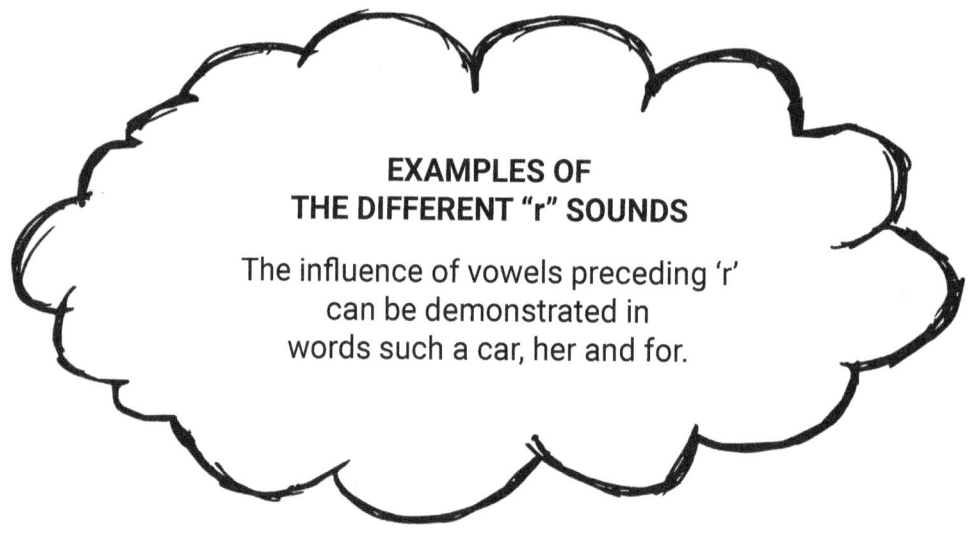

EXAMPLES OF THE DIFFERENT "r" SOUNDS

The influence of vowels preceding 'r' can be demonstrated in words such a car, her and for.

The 'ar' sound will be studied in the later section of final consonant sounds.

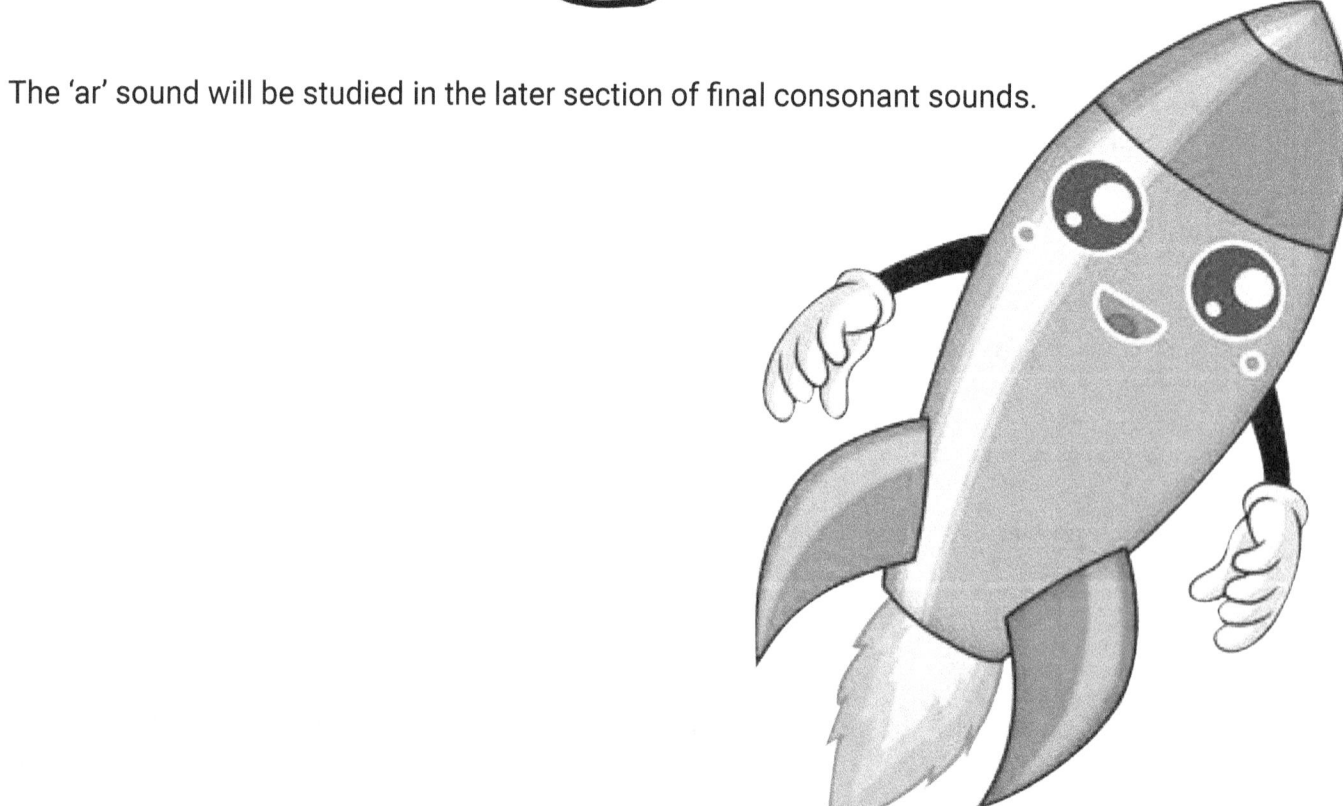

SUGGESTED WORDS AND PICTURES FOR THE FINAL "l" SOUND

sail bell fell tail wall tall table ball mail

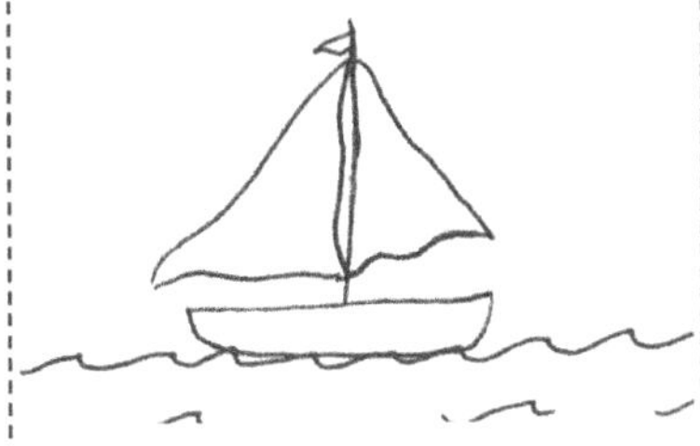
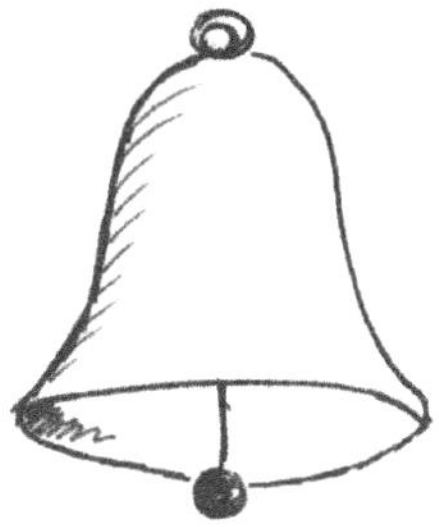
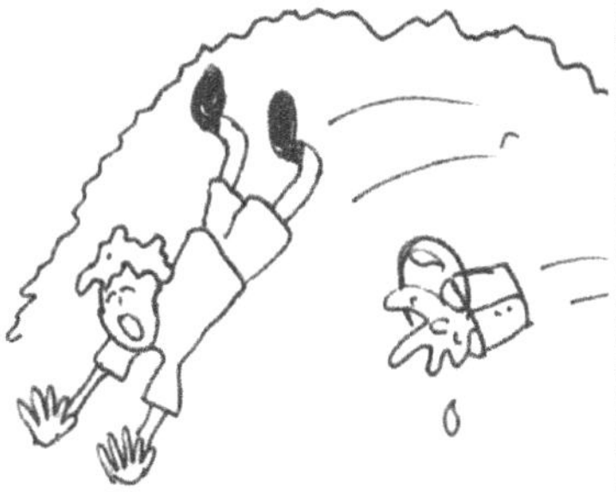
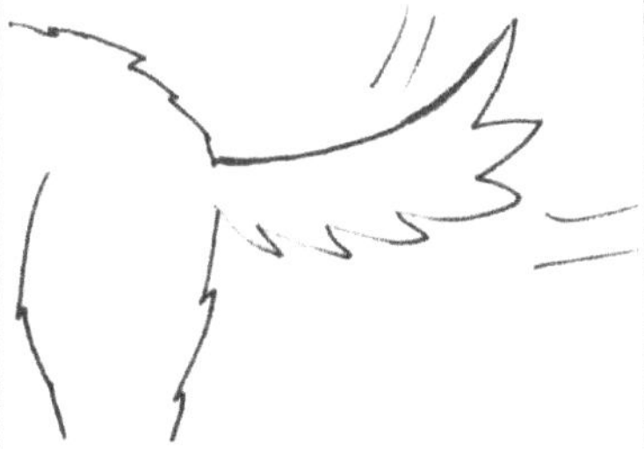
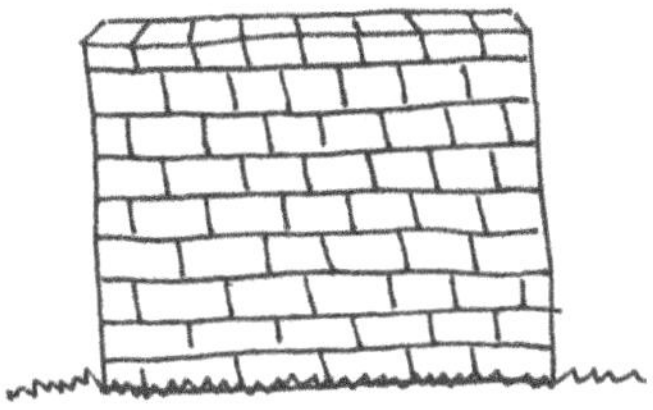
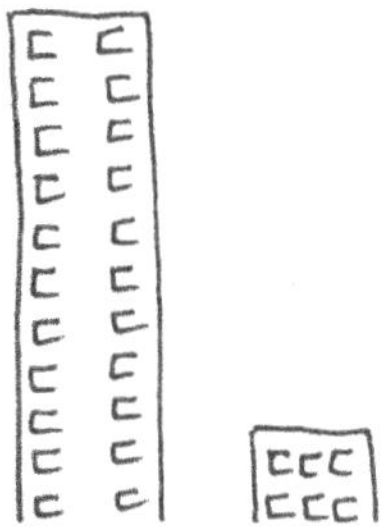
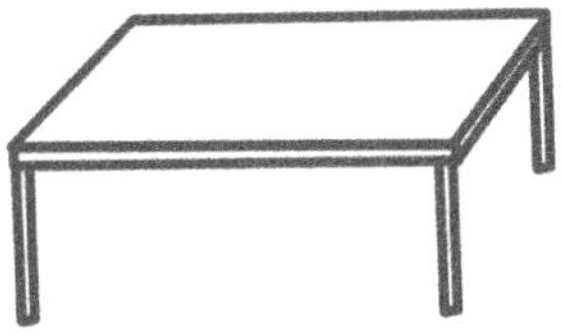
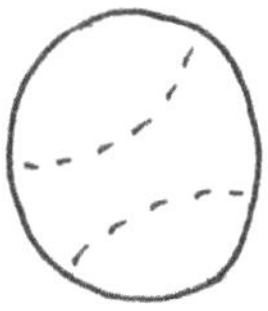
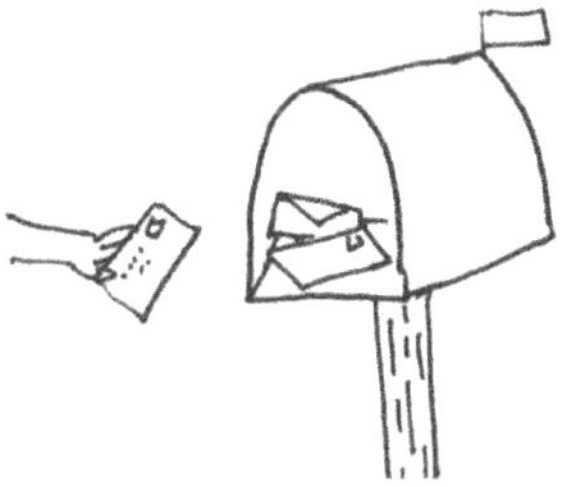

The blocks below may be cut and pasted next to pictures with final 'l', 'le' or 'll' spelling (sail, bell, fall, tail, wall, tall, ball, mail.) Once again it is the teacher's choice to use or not to use the written symbols. If the letters are used, direction will need to be given to ensure the correct end spellings match the pictures.

l	ll	ll	l	ll	ll	le	ll	l

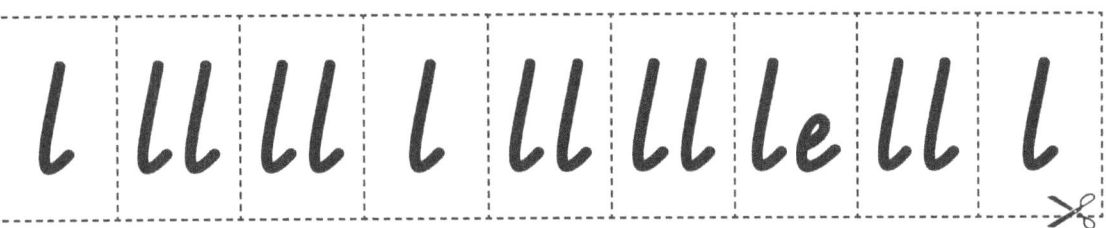

SUGGESTED PICTURES AND WORDS FOR THE IDENTIFICATION FINAL "f" SOUND

calf scarf laugh roof leaf cough

(If written symbols are used, remember do not paste the letter 'f' next to cough or laugh as this may cause confusion with later spelling)

| *f* | *f* | *gh* | *f* | *f* | *gh* |

PICTURES AND WORDS
FOR THE IDENTIFICATION FINAL "n" SOUND

sun bun run spin tin bin win pin ten

PICTURES AND WORDS FOR THE IDENTIFICATION FINAL "v" SOUND

glove   love   cave   save   brave   wave

| ve | ve | ve | ve | ve | ve |

SUGGESTED PICTURES AND WORDS FOR FOR THE IDENTIFICATION OF THE FINAL "z" SOUND

buzz nose snooze fuzz hose rose

| zz | se | ze | zz | se | se |

REVISION OF FINAL CONSONANTS

cave hose wave run school leaf cross pram mouse snooze worm bell

Final sustaining consonants in order of the following pictures: v, z, v, n, l, f, s, m, s, z, m, l.

SKILL

Identifying the different final sounds in the words corresponding with the following pictures.

INITIAL CONSONANT DIGRAPHS

This section may be regarded as a revision of the skills taught in the previous section, (Identification of the initial sound). The student is required to identify the target sound of the initial sounds 'sh', 'th' voiced, and 'th' voiceless and 'ch', aided by the use of pictures and articulation cues.

STUDENT OUTCOME
The student is encouraged to isolate and identify the initial sound in a word beginning with a consonant that has a continuous sound (called a continuant consonant).

METHOD
Follow the suggested lesson plans as detailed for identifying consonants in the initial position. With each new sound, substitute the new sound for the previously learned one. Say the words with an emphasis on the initial sound. **sh**ip, **sh**op

As pictures help to reinforce the short-term memory, my suggestion would be to use the pictures on the following page 55, before articulating the suggested words below. Some of these words do not have pictures, therefore one of the prompts has been withdrawn, making the task more difficult for beginning literacy learners.

SKILLS
Isolating and identifying the initial 'sh' sound using the following words and pictures.

EVALUATION
Competency is demonstrated when the student can identify and articulate the target sound from visual (picture) and oral (spoken) stimuli.

This lesson format may be used for the following lessons, that is, the identification of initial consonant digraphs (sounds), (two letter spelling choices).

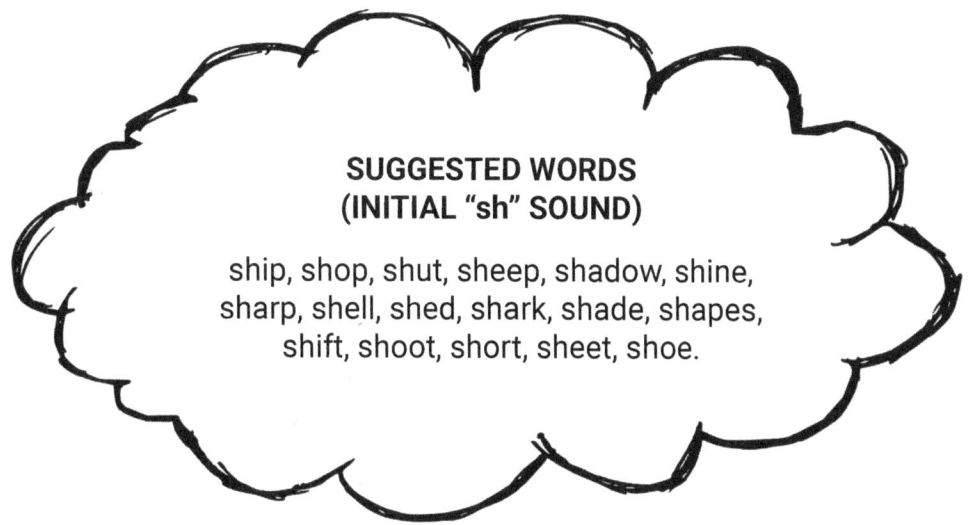

SUGGESTED WORDS (INITIAL "sh" SOUND)

ship, shop, shut, sheep, shadow, shine, sharp, shell, shed, shark, shade, shapes, shift, shoot, short, sheet, shoe.

SUGGESTED PICTURES FOR INITIAL CONSONANT DIGRAPH "sh"

ship shop sheep shadow shell shark shut shed shoe

sh | sh | sh | sh | sh | sh | sh | sh | sh

INITIAL VOICE CONSONANT DIGRAPH "th" SOUND

STUDENT OUTCOME

The student is encouraged to isolate and identify the initial sound in a word beginning with a consonant that has a continuous sound (called a continuant consonant).

This section may be regarded as a revision of the skills taught in the previous section, (Identification of the initial sound). The student is required to identify the target sound of the initial sounds 'sh', 'th' voiced, and 'th' voiceless and 'ch', aided by the use of pictures and articulation cues.

SUGGESTED WORDS FOR VOICED CONSONANT DIGRAPH "th"

As these words are difficult to illustrate with pictures, a discussion about their meanings and their use in sentences would be appropriate. The use of the actual objects rather than pictures would be more suitable. When articulating the word 'th ey', a sustained emphasis on the initial consonant, together with the correct hand cue should be sufficient for the student to isolate and identify this initial sound. The letters are included only if they are meaningful for the student (teacher's assessment).

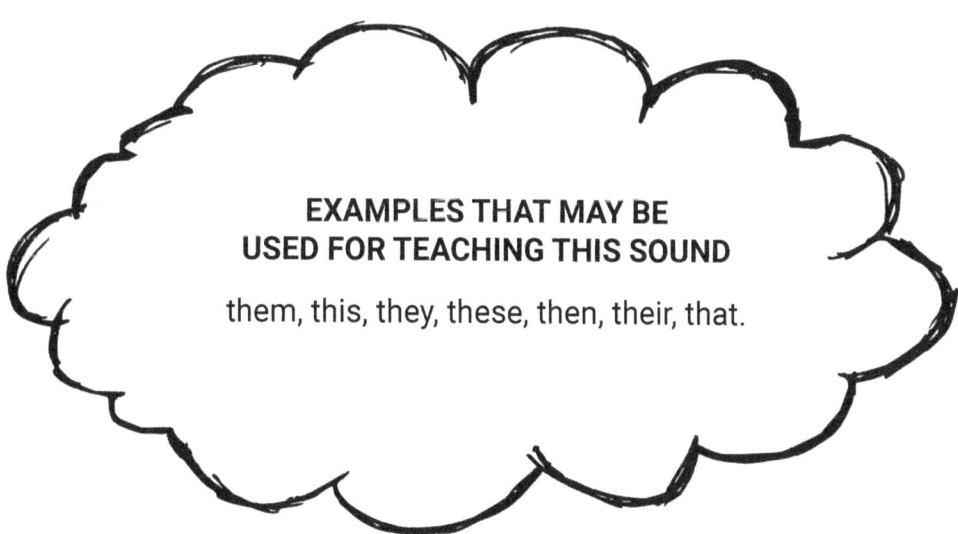

EXAMPLES THAT MAY BE USED FOR TEACHING THIS SOUND

them, this, they, these, then, their, that.

PICTURES FOR THE VOICED "th" SOUND IN THE INITIAL POSITION

__ __ em

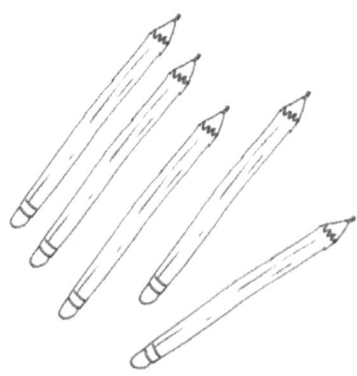

__ __ ese pencils

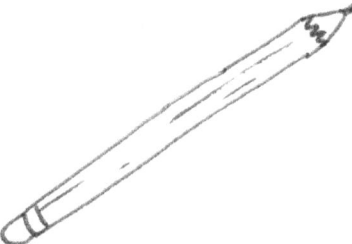

__ __ is way

__ __ at pencil

| th | th | th | th |

THE VOICELESS CONSONANT DIGRAPH "th" IN THE INITIAL POSITION

STUDENT OUTCOME, METHOD, EVALUATION

For the voiceless consonant digraph 'th' follow the previous lesson format as detailed for the voiced 'th' sound.

SUGGESTED WORDS

thick, thin, thread, thirsty, throne, third, thongs, thirty, think, throw, Thursday, threw, thunder, thief, thumb.

PICTURES FOR THE VOICELESS CONSONANT DIGRAPH "th" IN THE INITIAL POSITION

thong thick third thumb thin thirst

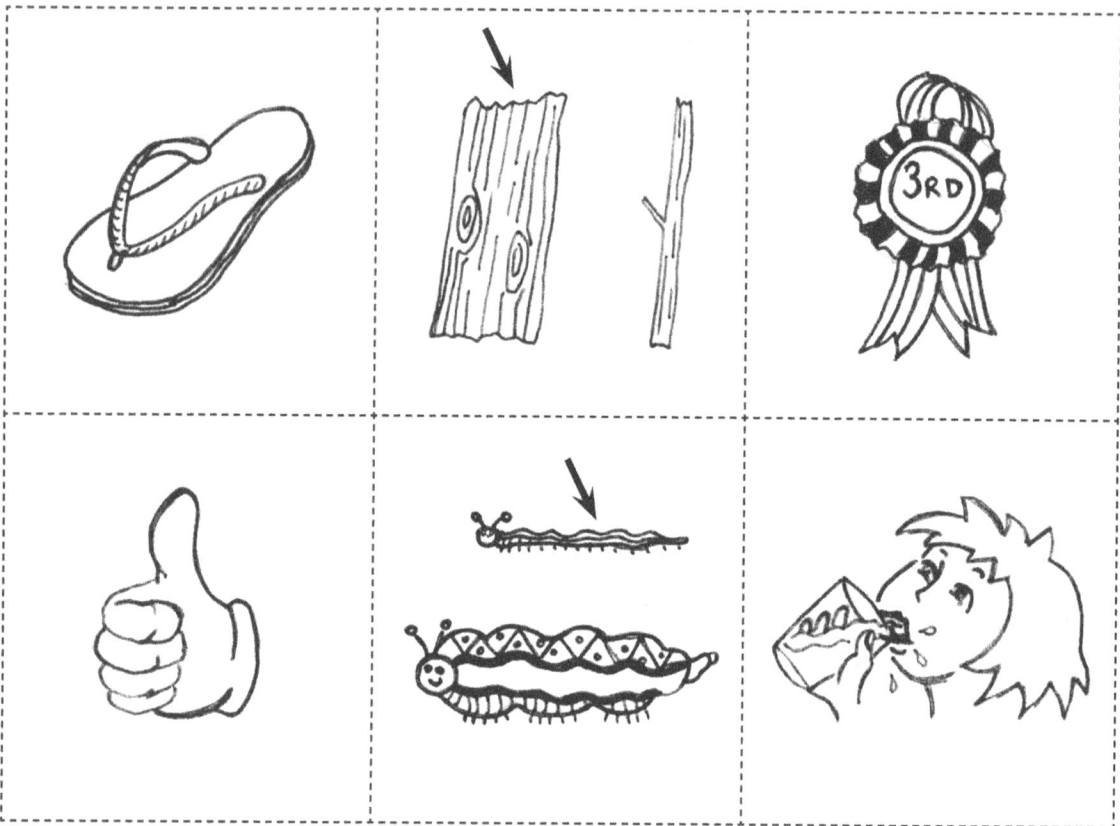

th *th* *th* *th* *th* *th*

THE VOICELESS CONSONANT DIGRAPH "ch" IN THE INITIAL POSITION

STUDENT OUTCOME (Consonant digraph "ch")

The student is encouraged to isolate and identify the initial sound in a word beginning with a consonant that has a continuous sound (called a continuant consonant).

METHOD AND EVALUATION

For the consonant digraph 'ch' in the initial position, follow the lesson format as detailed for the voiceless 'th' sound.

SKILL

Isolating and identifying the initial double consonant 'ch'.

EVALUATION

Competency in this skill is demonstrated when the student can correctly isolate the initial 'ch' sound from a list of 'ch' words and non 'ch' words.

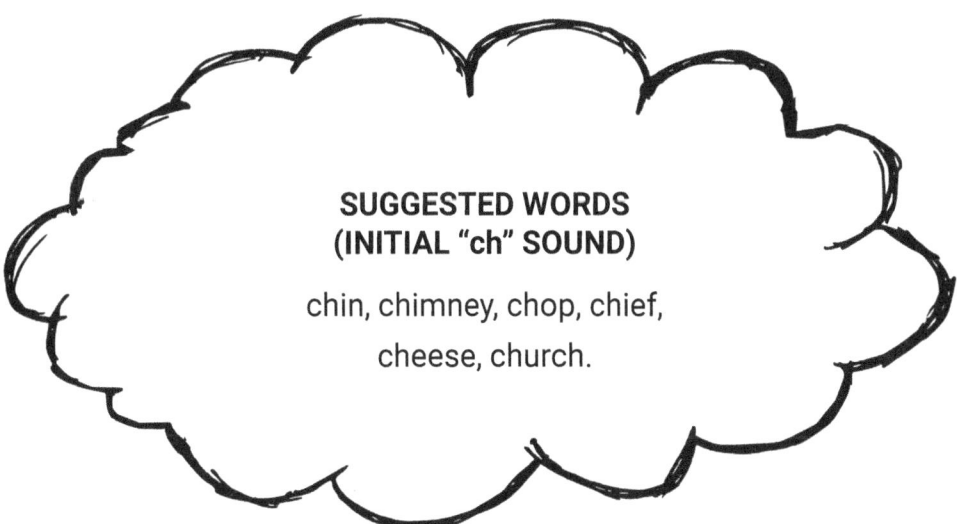

SUGGESTED WORDS (INITIAL "ch" SOUND)

chin, chimney, chop, chief, cheese, church.

The student may identify that the initial and final sound is the same in the word church, and if this is demonstrated the student is showing an acute auditory processing skill.

SUGGESTED PICTURES FOR INITIAL CONSONANT DIGRAPH "ch"

Cut out the 'ch' blocks below and place next to pictures with initial 'ch' spelling eg; church, chin, chimney, chop, chief, cheese.

| ch | ch | ch | ch | ch | ch |

FINAL CONSONANT SOUNDS

The lesson plan as detailed in the Segmentation Section for the Identification of Initial Consonant Sounds may be implemented for the final consonant and vowel sounds.

STUDENT OUTCOME

The student is encouraged to isolate and identify the final consonant or vowel sounds 'sh', 'ch', 'ow', 'y', 'oy', 'o' in the following lesson plans.

METHOD (As for final consonant sounds)

When saying these words remember that the emphasis is on the final sound, 'dish', 'fish', 'wash'.

SKILLS

Retaining in the short-term memory (with visual aids) the initial part of a word and then isolating and identifying the final target sound to complete the word. In the following lessons the final sounds listed above will be studied.

EVALUATION

Competency is achieved when the student demonstrates the ability to identify the target sound in a number of words with and without, the specific blend.

After working through both 'sh' groups, (that is 'sh' sound in both the initial and final positions) randomly select words from either group and encourage student to cue with the sign or clap, at the appropriate time when the targeted sound 'sh' is identified in each spoken word.

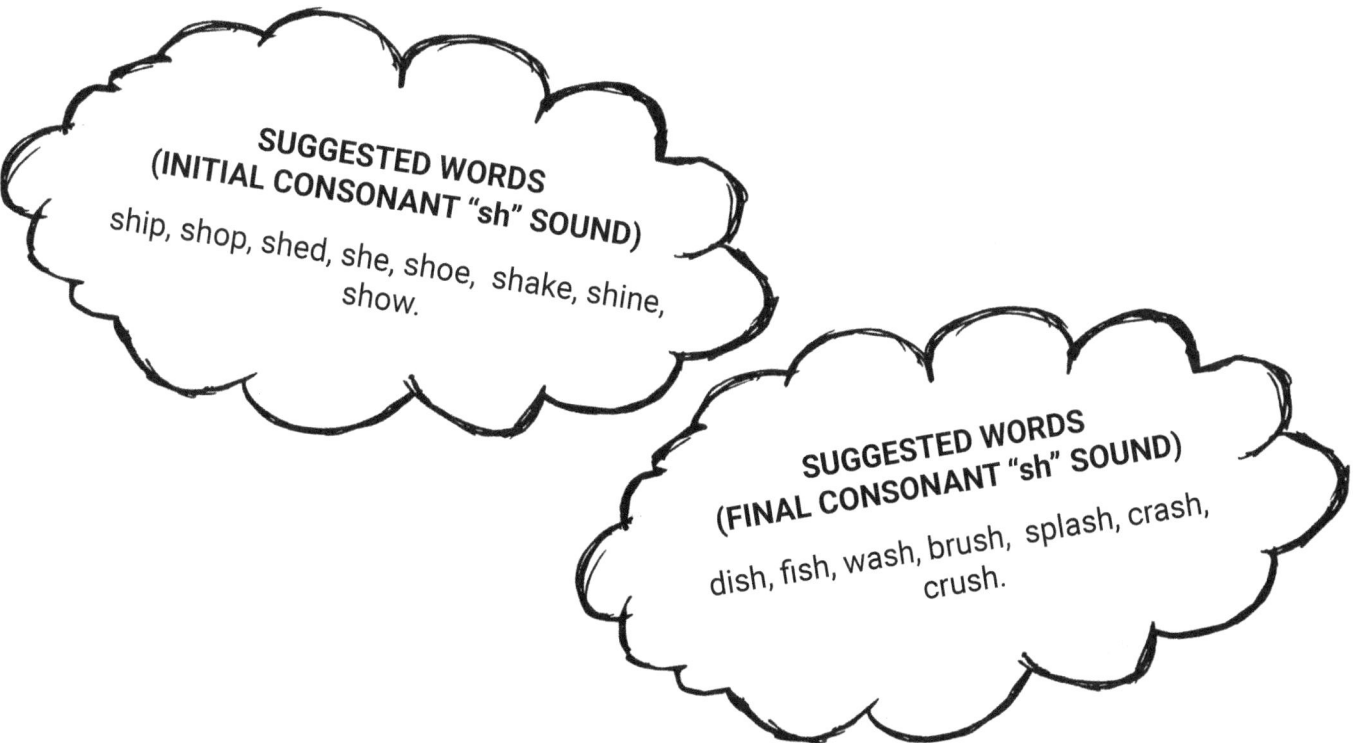

SUGGESTED WORDS
(INITIAL CONSONANT "sh" SOUND)
ship, shop, shed, she, shoe, shake, shine, show.

SUGGESTED WORDS
(FINAL CONSONANT "sh" SOUND)
dish, fish, wash, brush, splash, crash, crush.

SOME PICTURES FOR FINAL 'sh' SOUND

dish fish wash brush splash crash

sh | sh | sh | sh | sh | sh

CONSONANT DIGRAPH 'ch' IN THE FINAL POSITION

For the voiceless consonant digraph 'ch' in the final position, the Student Outcome, Method and Evaluation are the same as for the Segmentation Section with the only exception being that of substituting 'ch' for the previously taught final sound.

**SUGGESTED WORDS
(FINAL CONSONANT 'ch' SOUND)**

catch, patch, scratch, watch, perch, match, search, hatch, latch.

WORDS AND PICTURES FOR FINAL CONSONANT 'ch' AND 'tch'

catch patch scratch watch perch match beach hatch peach

If letters have been introduced, cut out the 'ch' blocks below and place next to pictures with final 'ch' spelling.

| tch | tch | tch | tch | ch | tch | ch | tch | ch |

THE VOWEL SOUND 'ow' IN THE FINAL POSITION

SUGGESTED LESSON PLAN

STUDENT OUTCOME
The student is encouraged to isolate and identify the initial sound in a word beginning with a consonant that has a continuous sound (called a continuant consonant).

METHOD AND EVALUATION
For the new phoneme 'ow' in the final position, follow the lesson format as detailed for the voiceless 'ch' sound.

SKILL
Isolating and identifying the final 'ow' sound in a number of picture words.

EVALUATION
As the teacher points to one of the 'ow' pictures and articulates the initial sound 'c' the student is encouraged to supply the final 'ow' sound. Alternatively the student may cue the 'ow' sound as the teacher/tutor articulates the word.

Repeat with other 'ow' pictures and additional words. If pictures are not available say, "Can you hear 'ow' in the word 'how', 'now', 'brow'?" Non-words may also be added, for example sprow, splow, dow, drow.

SUGGESTED WORDS AND PICTURES FOR 'ow' SOUND

cow bow sow plow/plough me-ow eyebrow

Cut out the 'ow' blocks below and place next to pictures with final 'ow' spelling.

THE VOWEL SOUND 'y' IN THE FINAL POSITION

STUDENT OUTCOME (Final vowel sound 'y' as in sky)
The student outcome is the same as for previously detailed final voiced phonemes, but once again substituting previously learned phonemes with the new vowel sound 'y' as in sky.

METHOD AND EVALUATION
Follow the same lesson plans as for previously learned phoneme in the final position.

SUGGESTED WORDS (FOR VOWEL 'y')

sky, high, my, sty, cry, fly, by/buy, dry, fry, why.

(Only use cut out letters for words ending in 'y').

SUGGESTED WORDS AND PICTURES FOR PHONEME 'y'

sky cry fly

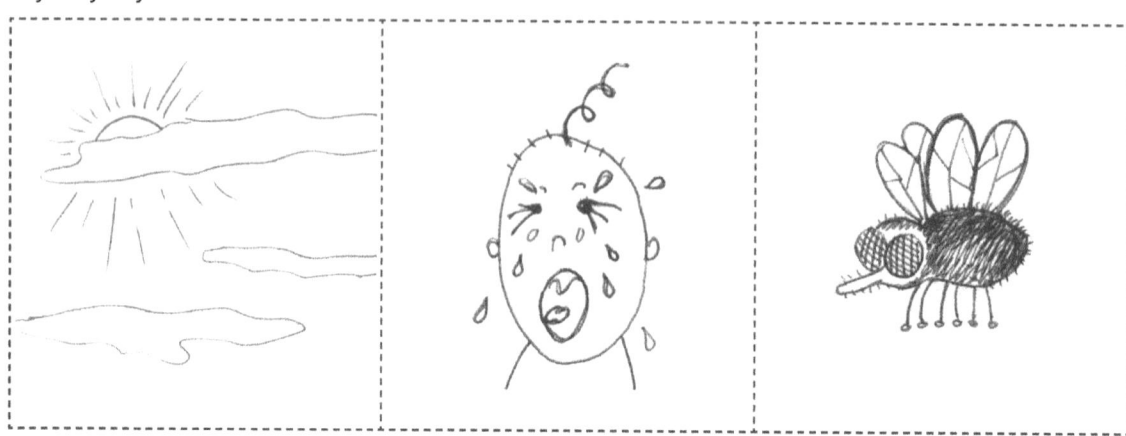

Cut out the 'y' blocks below and place next to pictures, also additional illustrations may be drawn for suggested words, with final 'y' spelling, for example sky, my, sty, cry, fly. The teacher may explain that 'high' uses other letters for this sound and if the student asks which letters are used the word 'high' may be written to illustrate the point.

y   y   y

THE VOWEL SOUND 'oy' IN THE FINAL POSITION

STUDENT OUTCOME (Initial and final sound 'oy' as in boy and oyster)
The Student outcome, Method and evaluation are the same as for previously detailed initial and final voiced phonemes, but once again substituting previously learned initial and final phonemes with the new sound 'oy' as in boy and oyster.

SUGGESTED WORDS AND PICTURES

(A clue such as 'the sound may not be at the end this time')

Cut out the 'oy' blocks below and place/paste next to pictures with final/initial 'oy' spelling, for example, boy, toy, Roy, destroy. The word 'oyster' has the target sound in the initial position and ointment has different letters to make the 'oy' sound, therefore if necessary, write the 'oi' letters if required.

| oy | oy | oy |

SUGGESTED WORDS AND SOME PICTURES FOR FINAL 'ar' SOUND

car star jar bar tar

ar   *ar*   *ar*

LONG VOWEL SOUND 'o' IN THE FINAL POSITION

STUDENT OUTCOME (final long vowel sound 'o' as in go)
The Student Outcome, Method and Evaluation are the same as for previously detailed final voiced phonemes, but once again substituting previously learned final phonemes with the new 'o' sound as in go. The teacher may choose to not use the 'ow' letters and just focus on the sound.

go ho-ho mo
(use cut out 'o' letters for these only, you may like to say that the other words have a different letter pattern, (that is 'ow')

crow blow flow
(and the different letter pattern may be used)

Cut out the letter blocks below and place next to pictures with final 'o' spelling eg; go, ho-ho and 'ow' spelling, for example, crow, blow, flow. Students may match appropriate endings and paste over final letter/letters of each word. Remember however that the primary purpose is the identification of sounds and the letter symbols may not be used until the student is in the second or third year of formal schooling.

STUDENT OUTCOME
(Long vowel sound 'a' as in angel)

The **student outcome**, **Method** and **evaluation** are the same as in Segmentation 1 (the isolation and identification of an initial phoneme) Coloured counters highlight the three distinct sounds in the word.

angel   ape   April   apron   apricot

Cut out the 'a' letter blocks below and place next to pictures with initial 'a' spelling eg; angle, ape, April, apron, apricot. Mention may be made that the upper case letters (or the letters that are like a keyboard) are used for names.

STUDENT OUTCOME
(Long vowel sound 'e' as in emu)

The **student Outcome**, **Method** and **Evaluation** are the same as in Segmentation 1 (the isolation and identification of an initial phoneme)

eagle   Easter   emu   eel

| ea | Ea | e | ee |

STUDENT OUTCOME
(Long vowel sound 'o' as in open)

Outcome Method and **Evaluation** are the same as in Segmentation 1 (the isolation and identification of an initial phoneme)

oval   open   over

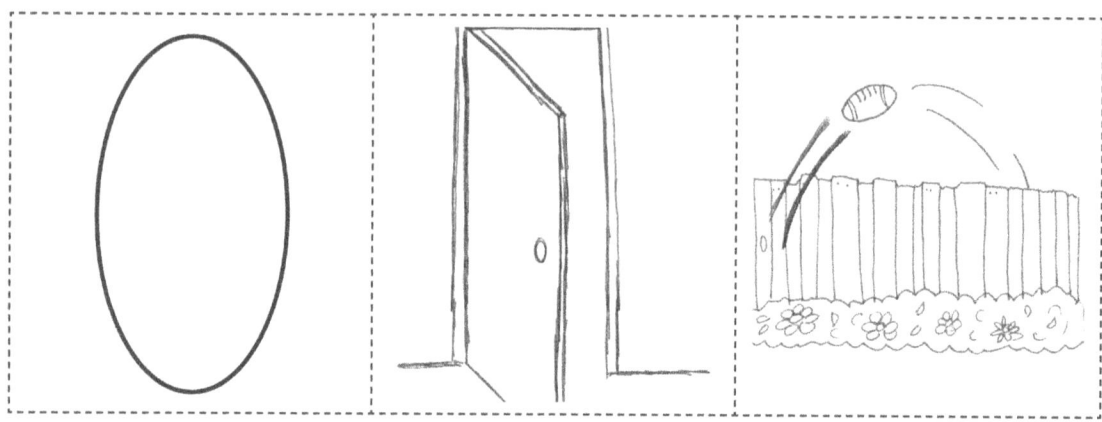

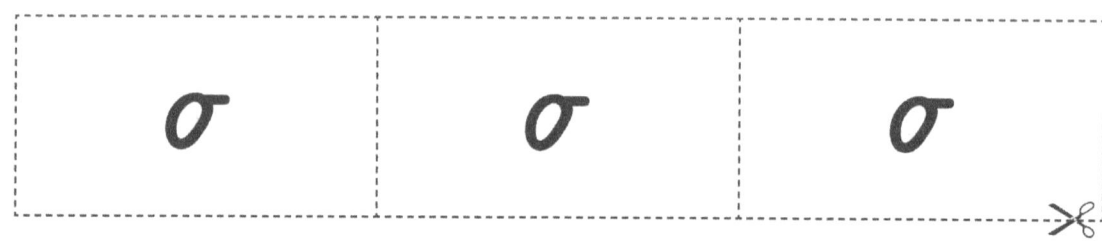

STUDENT OUTCOME
(Long vowel sound 'i' as in ice)

ice-cream   ice skating   ice block   icicle   iron   ibis

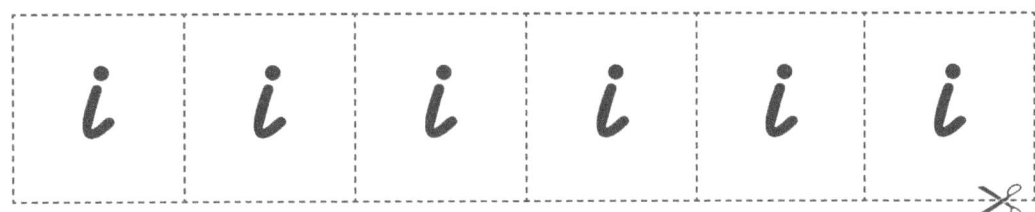

SHORT VOWELS

In this section the short vowels, a, e, i, o, u will be studied in the initial position and. appropriate words and some pictures will be given. The previously taught phonemes (sounds) have been of a nature that the sound can be sustained in both initial and final positions, thus facilitating a greater exposure to the **target** sound allowing for easier identifi cation and isolation.

Student Outcomes, **Method** and **Evaluation** will be the same as detailed in the sections Segmentation 1, identifying initial phoneme.

WORDS AND PICTURES FOR SHORT VOWEL 'a'

apple anchor ankle arrow axe ant

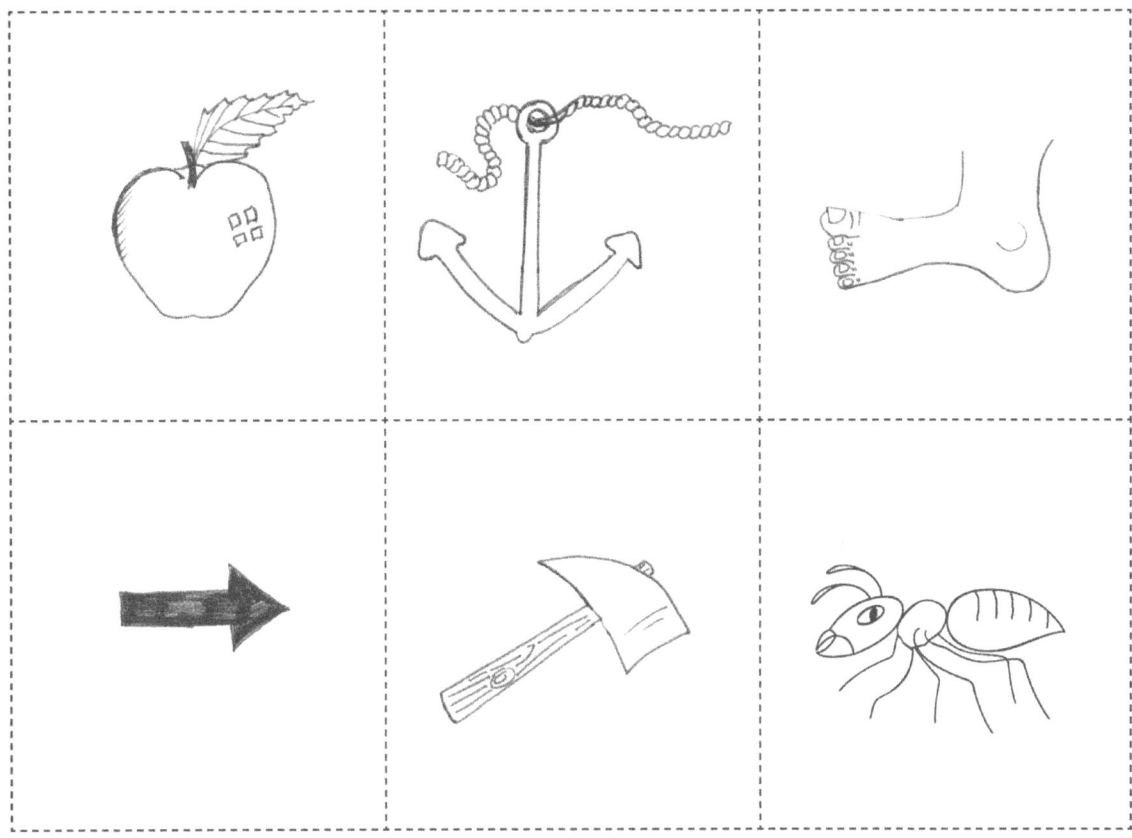

| *a* | *a* | *a* | *a* | *a* | *a* |

WORDS AND PICTURES FOR SHORT VOWEL 'e'

egg envelope elephant eggcup elbow engine

WORDS AND PICTURES FOR SHORT VOWEL 'i'

Indian igloo iguana insect ink inside

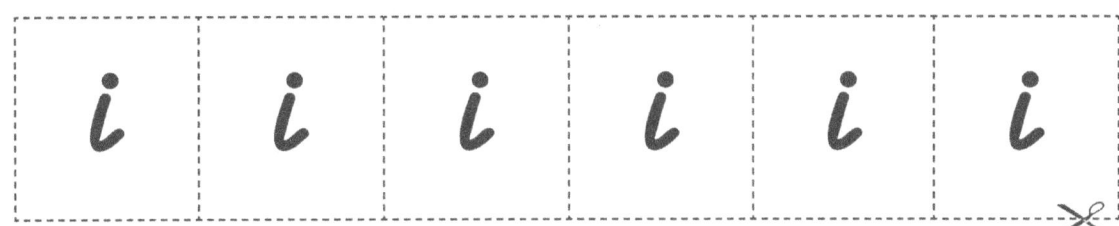

WORDS AND PICTURES FOR SHORT VOWEL 'o'

orange octopus octagon on ox ostrich

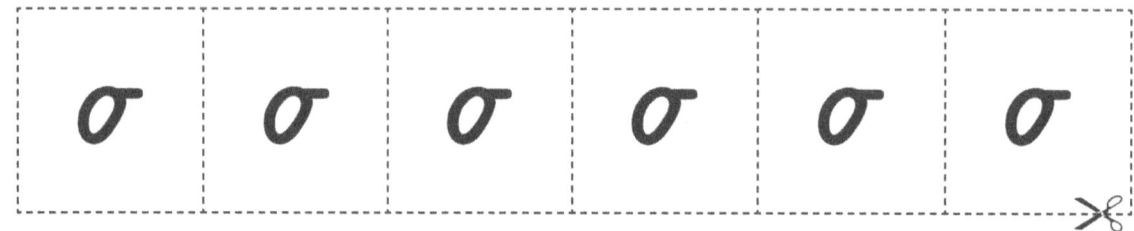

WORDS AND PICTURES FOR SHORT VOWEL 'u'

under umbrella ugly duckling umpire up undies

u u u u u u

IDENTIFICATION OF MEDIAL (MIDDLE) SOUND

The focus for this section is on the identification of the medial vowel in each spoken word. For this lesson it is the short vowel 'a' as in cat.

> ### STUDENT OUTCOME (Medial Sound 'a' as in ' cat')
> The student outcome is the same as for previously detailed final voiced phonemes, but once again substituting previously learned phonemes with the new vowel sound 'y' as in sky.

METHOD

Explain to the student that you are going to say a word slowly, but this time i would like you to listen and watch the speech organs (mouth, lips, teeth, tongue) and listen to the sound you hear when i clap.

With exaggerated lip movements slowly blend the sounds 'c-a-t' clapping on the middle sound. ask student to identify the sound he/she heard when you clapped.

Alternatively place three counters as the three sounds for 'cat' are articulated, then ask the student, "What sound did you hear for this counter?" pointing to the middle one.

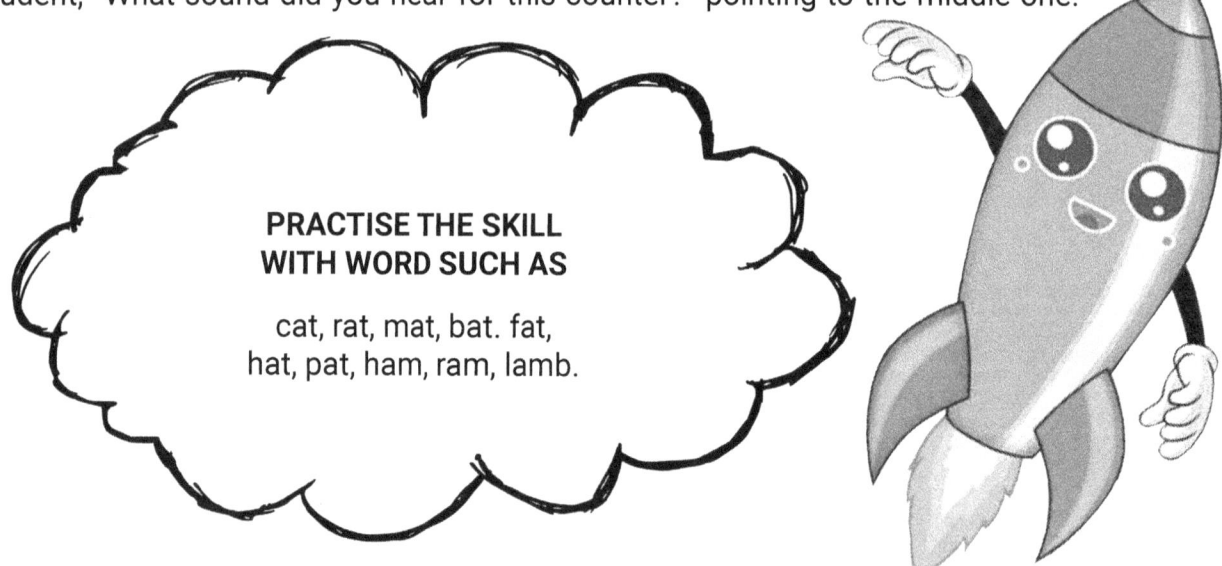

PRACTISE THE SKILL WITH WORD SUCH AS

cat, rat, mat, bat. fat, hat, pat, ham, ram, lamb.

Repeat words (plus any additional ones you can add). Encourage student to cue the 'a' sound as each word is slowly spoken. it may be appropriate for the tutor to write some of the words and color/underline the 'a' letter. The visual reinforcement (the written grapheme) may promote a beginning understanding of the concept that spoken sounds have their equivalent in written form.

EVALUATION

When the student correctly identifies the medial sound 'a' (as in cat) a number of times move on to the next short vowel sound, which may be one of the following: 'e, i, o, u'.

SUGGESTED WORDS AND PICTURES FOR MEDIAL SOUND 'a'

cat rat mat bat hat sat

SOME SUGGESTED WORDS AND PICTURES FOR MEDIAL SHORT VOWEL 'e' SOUND

(Remember it is helpful to construct a meaningful sentence for each picture.) Counters may be used as in the previous lesson.

pet jet net ten hen men pen wet bed

SUGGESTED WORDS AND PICTURES FOR SHORT MEDIAL SOUND 'i'

Continue to use counters if these help the students to isolate the middle sound.

tin bin fin pin win sit hit sip lip

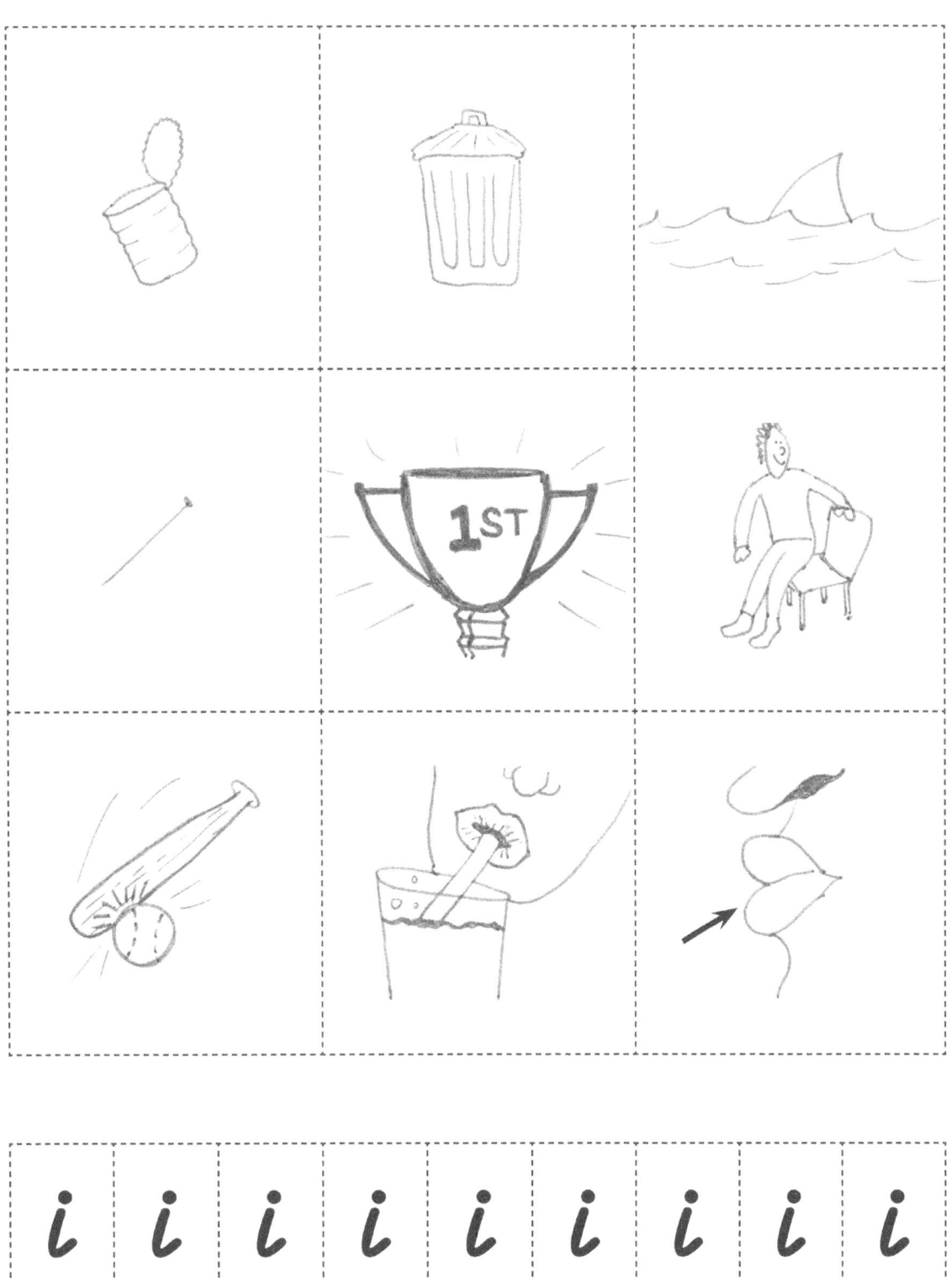

SUGGESTED WORDS AND PICTURES FOR SHORT MEDIAL SOUND 'o'

hot dot cot hop top mop pop pot tot

o	o	o	o	o	o	o	o	o

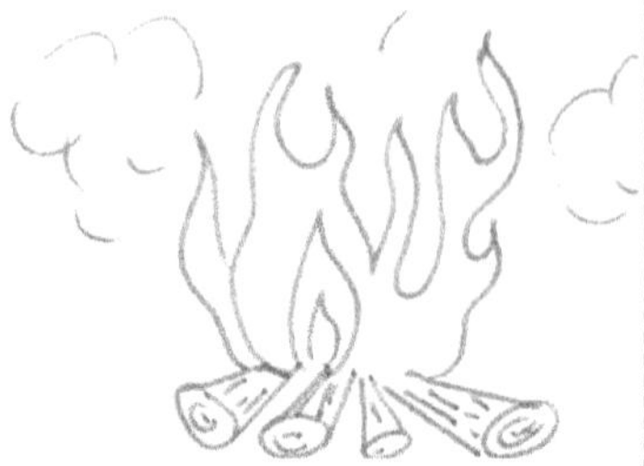

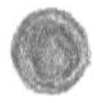

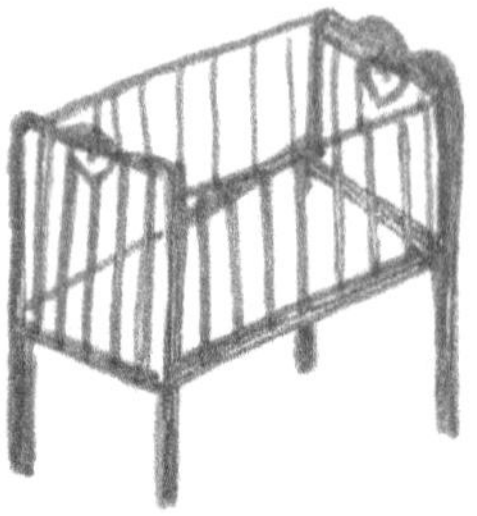

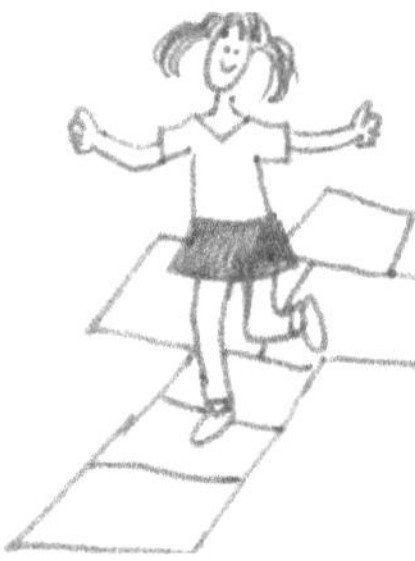

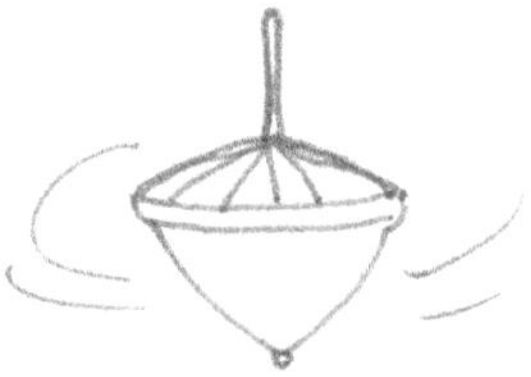

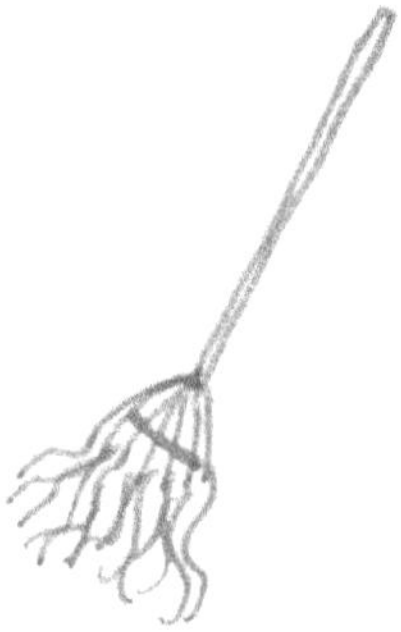

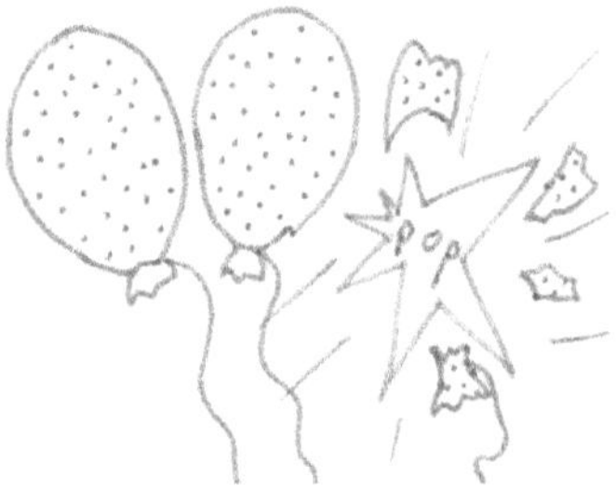

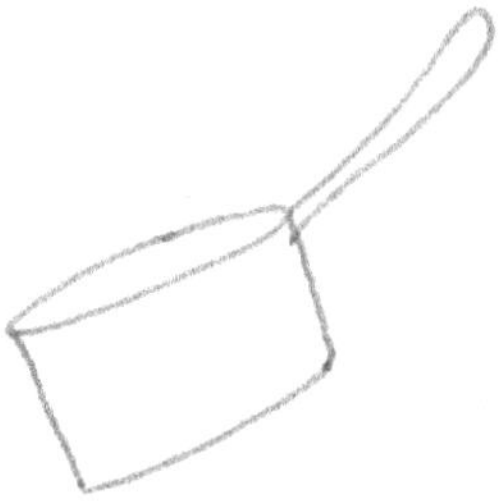

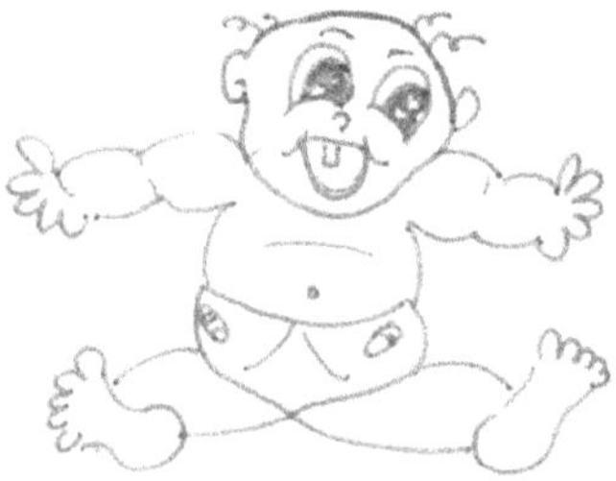

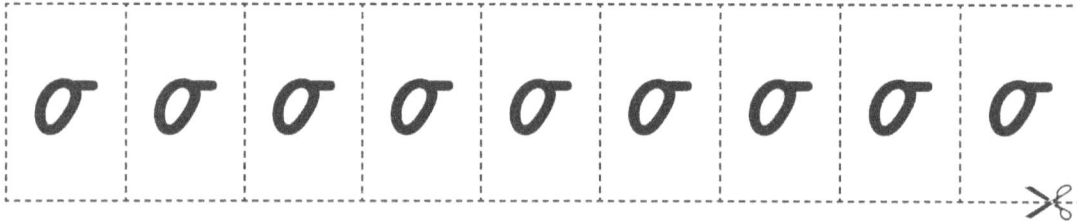

SUGGESTED WORDS AND PICTURES FOR MEDIAL SOUND 'u'

hut nut cup pup run sun bun mum sum

REMAINING SOUNDS IN INITIAL AND FINAL POSITIONS IN WORDS

The remainder of the consonants may be taught using previously detailed formats. it is not necessary to conform to the suggested order for teaching the remaining sounds as these sounds appear to be of a similar degree of difficulty for beginning readers. The remaining sounds are articulated in a more abrupt manner, that is, they do not contain the sustaining qualities of previously taught sounds, and for this reason the auditory identification task becomes more difficult.

Students, at this stage, should be encouraged to identify sounds in both the initial and final positions and where necessary in the medial or middle positions.

Remaining sounds to be taught using this manual are as follows:

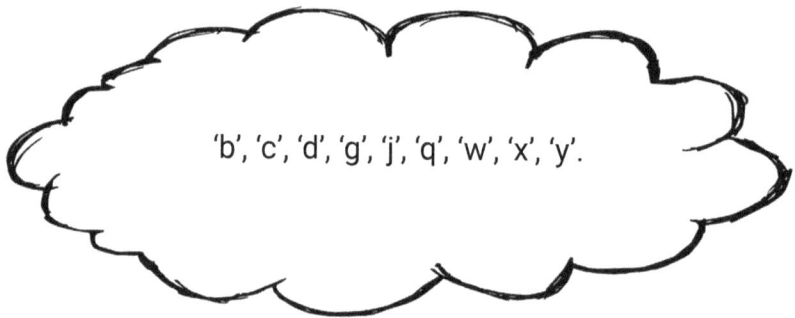

'b', 'c', 'd', 'g', 'j', 'q', 'w', 'x', 'y'.

The following consonants are voiceless, but the restriction of the wind passage by the lips or the tongue produce a small explosive or popping sound:

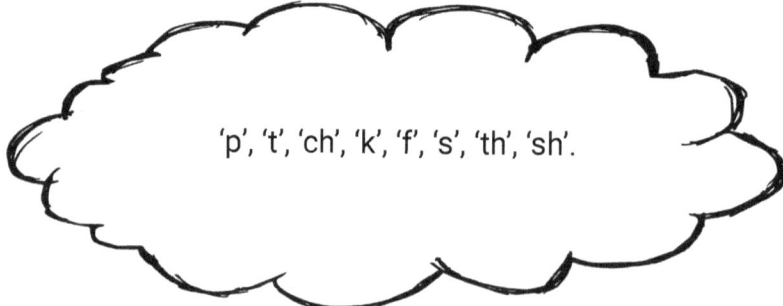

'p', 't', 'ch', 'k', 'f', 's', 'th', 'sh'.

With the exception of the first two sounds, the remaining sounds have been previously taught in either the initial position and or the final position in words.

The remaining sound 'h' is an unimpeded voiceless sound, and may be called the puffing sound.

PICTURES FOR WORDS CONTAINING THE VOICED 'b' SOUND

bat ball beach basket balloon butterfly

(*final sound*) **crab tub cub**

The pictures for the end sound 'b' may be identified with a circle to signify their difference from the other pictures.

PICTURES FOR WORDS CONTAINING THE 'k' SOUND (LETTER C)

cow can candle camel crab clock clown computer cat

c c c c c c c c c

PICTURES FOR WORDS CONTAINING THE 'd' SOUND

dog duck dinosaur dolphin deer dig diamond dance dart

d d d d d d d d d

PICTURES FOR WORDS CONTAINING THE 'g' SOUND

goat girl goose gorilla golf guitar

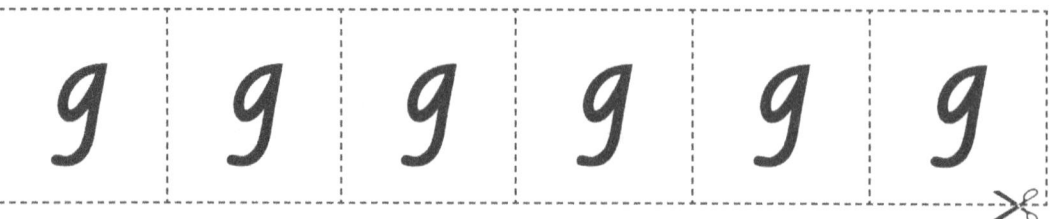

PICTURES FOR WORDS CONTAINING THE 'j' SOUND

jelly jet jellyfish jump jellybeans jumper jug jar jog

j j j j j j j j j

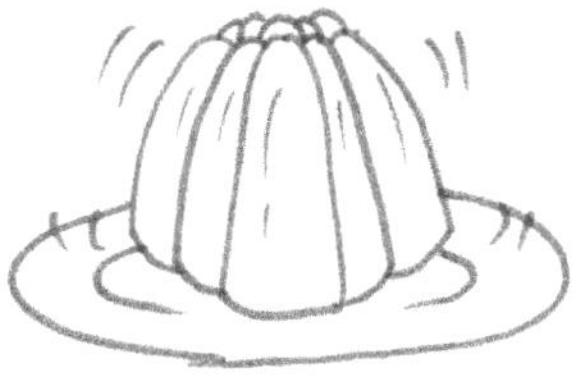

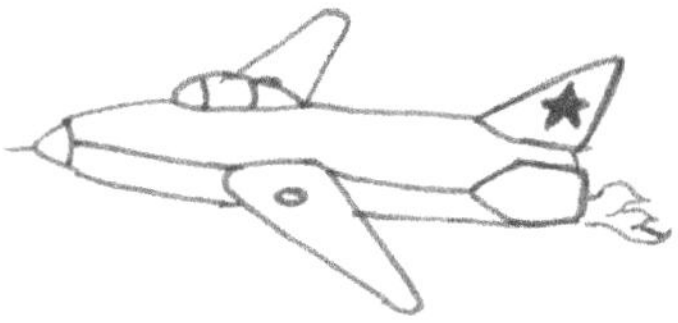

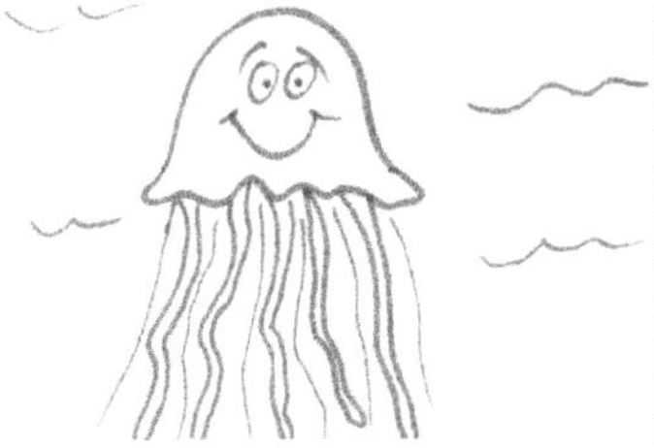

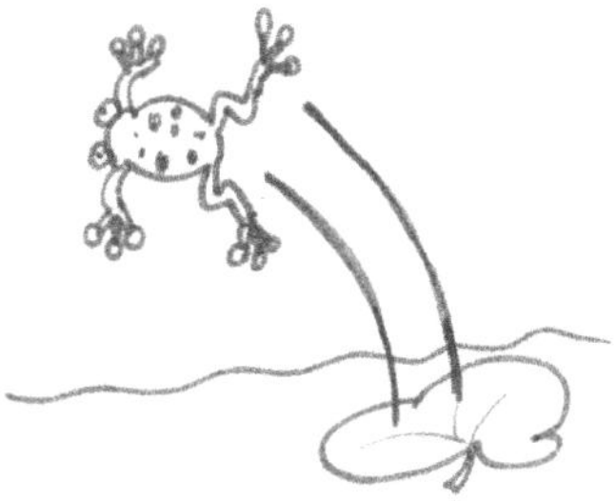

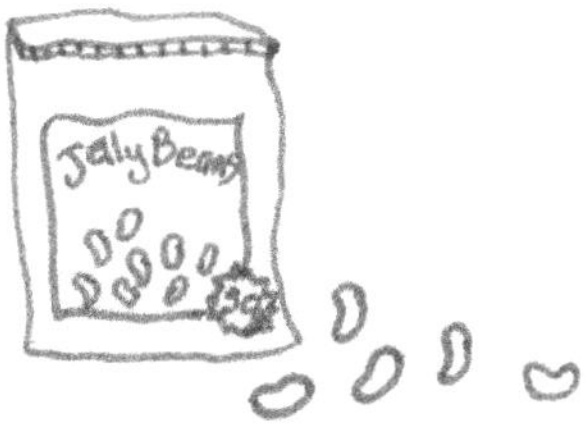

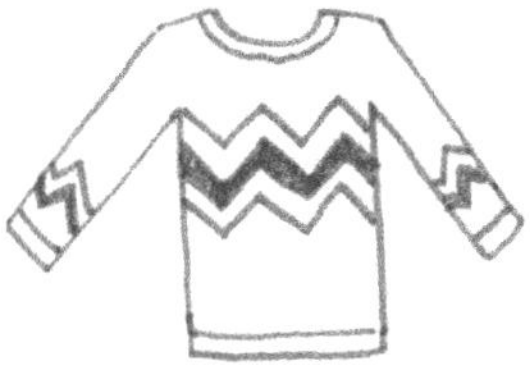

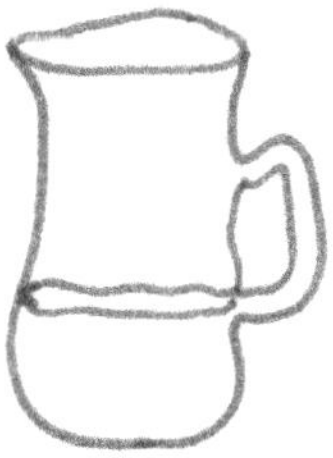

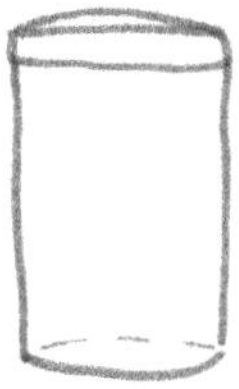

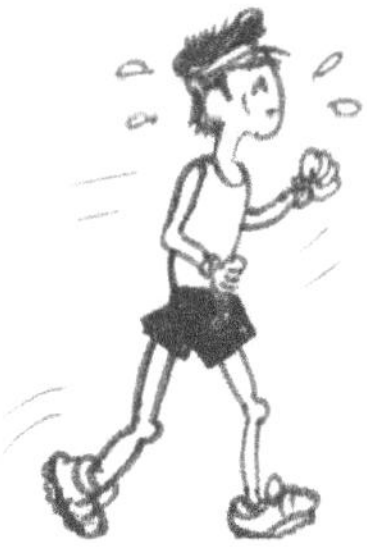

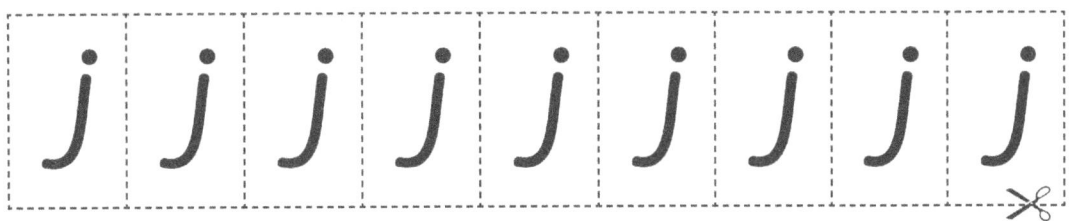

PICTURES FOR WORDS CONTAINING THE 'q' SOUND

This sound is made by quickly blending 'k' and 'w'. This may be demonstrated by showing the two different positions of the speech organs and the two hand cues, as the sound is pronounced. thus, 'qu' is a consonant blend as two speech sounds are being produced.

queen   quill   quail   question   quilt   quarter

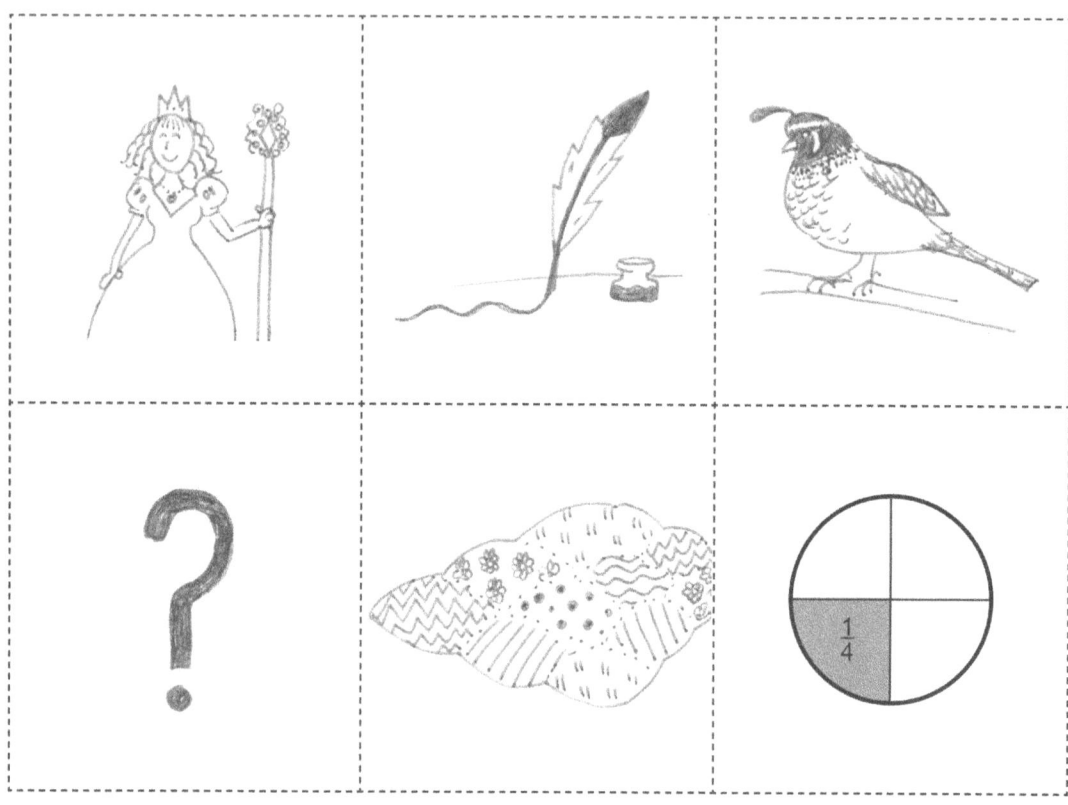

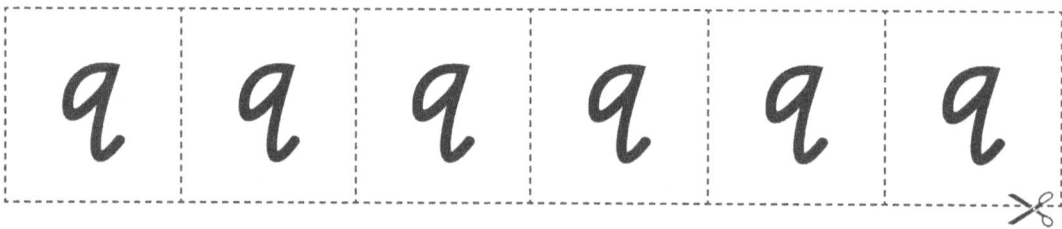

PICTURES FOR WORDS CONTAINING THE 'w' SOUND

windmill   watch   wave   window   wallaby   wolf   whistle   whale   wedding

PICTURES FOR WORDS CONTAINING THE 'x' SOUND

The 'x' sound is a combination of the 'k' and 's' sounds, both of which have been taught separately in previous lessons. encourage students to watch as the speech organs change position, and also demonstrate the two hand cues. For this sound the words and pictures will illustrate the phoneme in the final position.

box   fox   six

PICTURES FOR WORDS CONTAINING THE 'y' SOUND

yacht yawn yell yabbie yo-yo yak

VOICELESS CONSONANT SOUNDS

The next group of consonants are voiceless sounds 'p', 't', 'k', 'f', 's', 'h', 'sh', 'ch' and 'th' (this sound may also be a voiced sound as in 'this'.) Some of these sounds have been previously taught with the continuant consonant sounds.

The consonant digraph sound 'sh' was also studied in the previous section of continuant consonants.

Voiceless sounds, as the name suggests, do not use the voice but depend on the position of the speech organs to make the sound. Students should therefore, be encouraged to notice the particular positions of the speech organs especially the lips and tongue.

The use of the Cued Articulation signs may be particularly helpful for these sounds because of their voiceless nature

PICTURES FOR WORDS CONTAINING THE VOICELESS 'p' SOUND

pig   pin   pot   panda   penguin   pizza   pen   pencil   paper

PICTURES FOR WORDS CONTAINING THE VOICELESS 't' SOUND

top tin tiger turtle table teddy teeth toaster toes

PICTURES FOR WORDS CONTAINING THE INITIAL VOICELESS 'k' SOUND

kite kitten key king kick kiwi kangaroo koala kennel

This will be a revision of the 'k' sound as it was taught with 'c' letter words

PICTURES FOR WORDS CONTAINING THE VOICELESS 'th' SOUND

thick   thirsty   third   thong   thin   thumb

| *th* | *th* | *th* | *th* | *th* | *th* |

PICTURES FOR WORDS CONTAINING THE VOICELESS 'h' SOUND

horse house hut hill heart hat hand hair hot

BLENDING

Blending is an important process in the pre-reading stage. It is a process of combining a sequence of sounds to produce a word. This is purely an auditory process at this stage.

Children can be introduced to blending as soon as they know a small group of sounds.

Smooth and effortless blending is important in later reading skills. a brief revision of previously taught sounds may assist in an automatic recognition of single sounds prior to learning blending skills.

The blending process is introduced using two letter words that contain a vowel and a consonant, (vc) or a consonant, vowel (cv) pattern. After practising this skill with two sounds, move on to words with three sounds.

SUGGESTED TWO SOUNDED WORDS

Two letters and two sounds: at, am, an, in, it, on, up, us, my, by. three or four letters but still two sounds: add, off, tie, pie, high. three or four letters but still two sounds: add, off, tie, pie, high.

IDENTIFICATION OF MEDIAL (MIDDLE) SOUND

The objective of any phonemic activity should be the identification of a particular sound/s. Blending requires the skill of identifying then blending two or more sounds to articulate a particular word.

STUDENT OUTCOME

the student is encouraged to successfully identify and retain in their short-term memory, two individual phonemes that are then blended to form a word.

METHOD

Tell the student that you are going to say two sounds that make a little word.

Explain to the student that your lips change shape with the different sounds and encourage the student to watch for these changes.

Say 'a–t' as you move two counters into the boxes below and then ask the student, "What little word did you hear me say?" The quick response should be 'at'

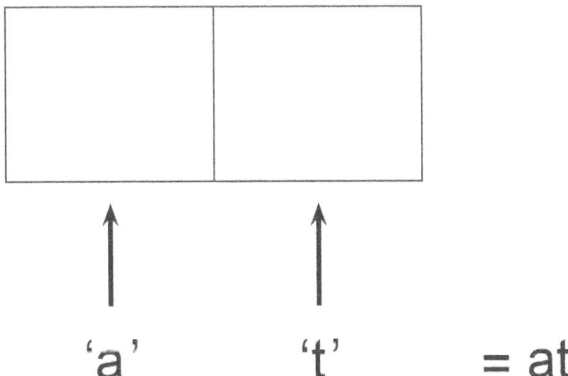

The teacher articulates the two sounds suggested in the two letter words on the previous page as the counters are moved into the boxes and the student blends to identify the words.

Now tell the student that you are going the say words that tell you something. This is called a sentence. Use sentences beginning with 'at', and articulate the beginning word with a slight emphasis. Ask the student to tell you the first word in the sentence. Repeat with a number of different simple sentences. The suggested words on the previous page may be used. The student may clap when the target word is pronounced.

EVALUATION

The student is competent in this skill when he/she can correctly identify the two sounded sequence, and blend the sounds to form the target word.

SKILL

identifying and blending two separate sounds to form a word.

SUGGESTED SENTENCES

Firstly students are asked to identify the first word in a sentence, then the target word in other positions within a sentence.

Also encourage student to make sentences with suggested two sounded words.

At the beach we played in the sand.

Am I going too?

An orange is orange.

Add the lollies together. how many are there?

In the bag you can find your book.

It is a hot day.

off you run.on the table, find your pencil.

Up the steps you go.

Come with **us**.

This is **my** book

Walk **by** the shops.

The man has a **tie**.

My Mum makes a meat **pie**.

That is a **high** building.

SKILL

Identifying two sounded words at the beginning and also submerged in sentences.

EVALUATION

Competency is demonstrated when the student identifies and signals when the target word is spoken.

Students may now be ready to blend three sounded words.

On the following pages some pictures will be given, as visual support, to emphasize the target word in the short-term memory. As the blending skill is increasingly practiced students should not need the visual reinforcement.

The teacher demonstrates by slowly articulating each sound that makes up the word, whilst at the same time pushing the counters into the boxes, (this signifies the number of sounds that the student needs to retain). The student then blends all sounds, pronounces the word and points to the picture.

At this stage the three sounds will match the word for the picture.

As the student becomes familiar with the process, three sounded words without pictures may be introduced.

BLENDING (continued)

SUGGESTED WORDS FOR BLENDING PRACTICE

The teacher says, 'i–t', student blends and says, 'it'. The student is encouraged to retain the 'it' word rather than articulating both sounds.

'It' words may now be practised, with the teacher pronouncing each word slowly, firstly saying the onset 's' and then the rime 'it'. The student then blends and says the word, for example sit, lit, fit, mit, hit, kit, pit, bit, wit. Extra practice may be given with nonsense words, for example zit, vit, rit, nit, srit, plit, crit, smit.

Suggested words and nonsense words for blending and identifying the 'an' rime: The teacher says, 'a' 'n' student says, 'an'. Follow the method as suggested above.

Words and nonsense 'an' words for practice maybe: dan, ban, fan, tan, van, can, man, nan, pan, ran, scran, plan, slan, han, gran.

Suggested 'am' words and nonsense words for blending and identifying the 'am' rime: Sam, dam, ham, jam, Pam, ram, pram, tram, stam, cram, lamb (remember the focus is only to identify the 'am' sound and blend it with the onset 'l').

Extra practice may be given with onsets of three consonants, for example stram, strat.

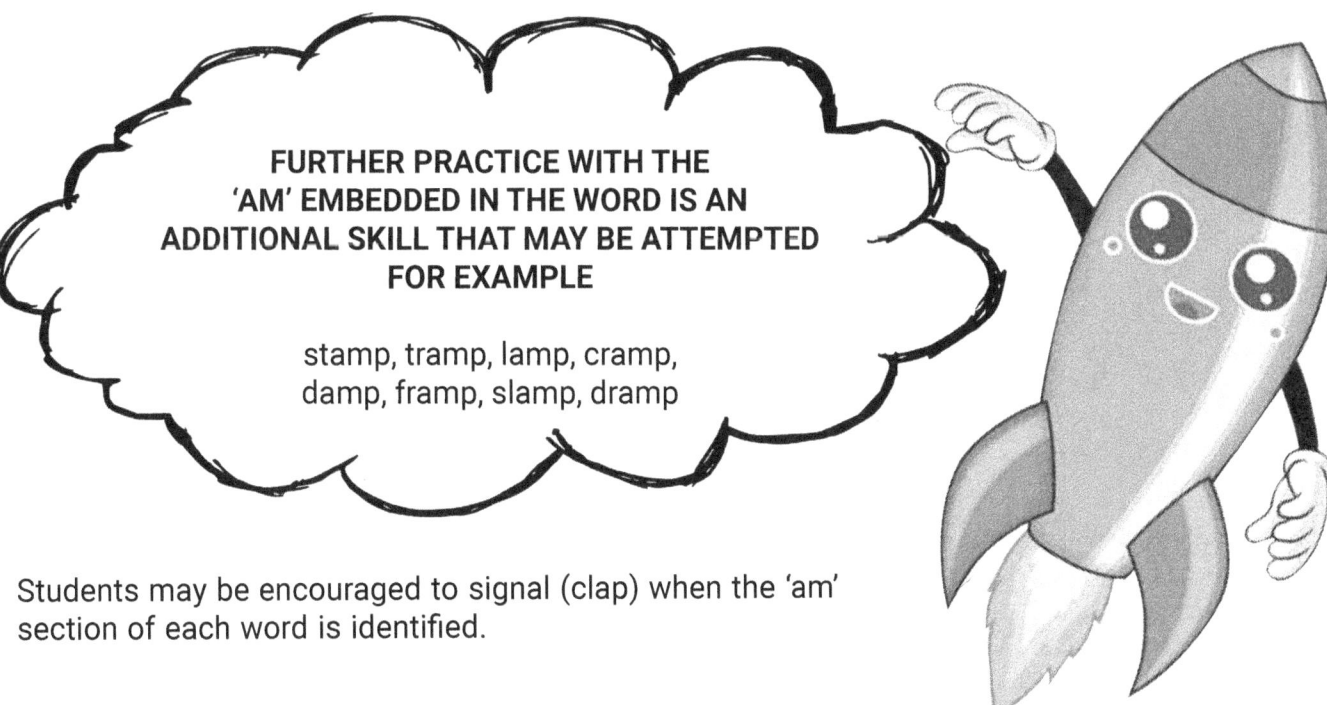

FURTHER PRACTICE WITH THE 'AM' EMBEDDED IN THE WORD IS AN ADDITIONAL SKILL THAT MAY BE ATTEMPTED FOR EXAMPLE

stamp, tramp, lamp, cramp, damp, framp, slamp, dramp

Students may be encouraged to signal (clap) when the 'am' section of each word is identified.

BLENDING (continued)

WORDS WITH 'AT' BLEND

cat   rat   bat   sat

SKILL

Blending 'a' 't' sounds to make words, with and without reference to visual stimuli.

BLENDING (continued)

WORDS WITH 'OT' BLEND

cot dot hot pot not lot rot tot

SKILL

Blending 'o' 't' sounds to make words, with and without reference to visual stimuli.

PICTURES FOR BLENDING 'it' WORDS

WORDS WITH 'IT' BLEND

sit hit lit fit bit kit pit

SKILL

Blending 'i' 't' sounds to make words, with and without reference to visual stimuli.

PICTURES FOR BLENDING 'an' WORDS

WORDS WITH 'AN' BLEND

man fan pan ran dan tan van

SKILL

Blending 'a' 'n' sounds to make words, with and without visual stimuli.

SUGGESTED 'in' WORDS FOR BLENDING PRACTICE

Suggested 'in' words and nonsense words for blending and identifying the 'in' rime:

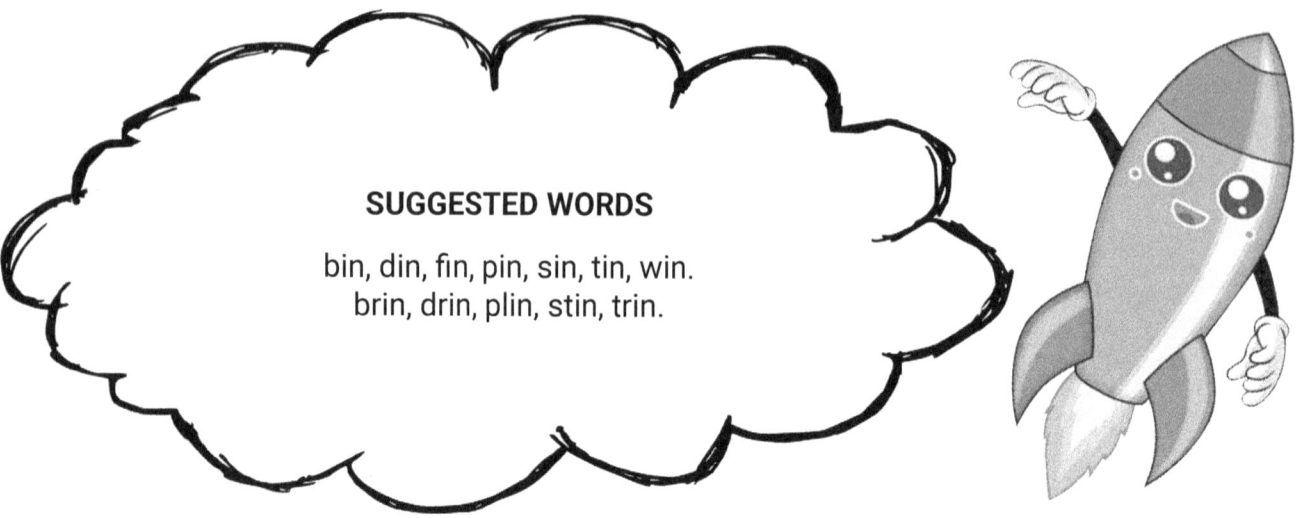

SUGGESTED WORDS

bin, din, fin, pin, sin, tin, win.
brin, drin, plin, stin, trin.

Students may identify the 'in' words in the following sentences by an appropriate action, for example, clapping when they hear the target word 'in', in each sentence.

In the **bin** i found a **pin**.

The **tin** is in the **bin**.

By the **bin** i saw a **fin**.

I can **win** a race.

A **sin** is doing something wrong.

I saw a fish **fin** in the **bin**.

The **tin** and the **bin** made a **din**.

SUGGESTED WORDS FOR BLENDING 'on' WORDS

Suggested 'on' words and nonsense words for blending and identifying the 'on' rime. At this early stage of beginning literacy skills, the rime section may be slightly emphasised to assist the acquisition of blending skills.

A suggested activity may be for the teacher to say a number of words with the 'on' rime and a number of words minus the 'on' rime. The student claps (taps, stands up) when an 'on' word is spoken. The following 'ready-made' lists may be useful.

House, car, Don, pram, hat, dad, play, Ron. "How many words had the 'on' bit?"

Swim, slon, jump, tree, cron, boy, hat, run, clon, bron, cup. "How many claps did you make?"

D–on, R–on,

S–t–on, f–r–on, p–r–on, s–l–on, b–r–on, c–l–on, c–r–on.

Sentences to assist in identifying the 'on' rime.

Appropriate actions may be performed each time an 'on' word is identified, for example, hands up, then hands down, hands up. Continue throughout the story.

> **Don** is a small boy, and he has a friend called **Ron**. **Don** and **Ron** like to play together. **Don** loves to play football, but **Ron** likes to play basketball.
>
> **Ron's** mum is called **Bron** and **Don's** mum is called **Fron**.
>
> **Don's** dad's name is **Slon**, and **Ron's** dad is called **Stron**.
>
> So that makes the 'on' families of **Don, Ron, Fron, Slon** and **Stron**.

What funny names they have!

The student may choose to draw the families and practise saying the families' names.

SUGGESTED WORDS FOR BLENDING THE 'up' RIME

Suggested words and nonsense words for blending and identifying the 'up' rime:

The teacher may use the pictures for the first two words as a prompt to assist the student retain the on-set in the short term memory whilst blending the rime section to complete the word 'cup'.

The teacher clearly articulates the onset 'c' then the rime 'up', student blends for 'cup'.

C–up, p–up, s–up, m–up, l–up, n–up, v–up, r–up, t–up.

extra practice may be given with some nonsense words C-r-up, p-r-up, s-l-up, c-l-up.

BLENDING (continued)

An extension of the three sounds, three letter words may now be the three sounded words with four or more letters. i.e. The words still only employ three sounds.

As in previous lessons the teacher articulates individual sounds in each word and the student blends to identify each word.

Words such as house, tree, truck, train, boat.

Some students may now be ready to move to regular words with four sounds.

Sand, hand, band, went, sent, bent, rest, best, west, and test.

The sound boxes may still be used to illustrate the number of sounds the student needs to identify and blend to form a word.

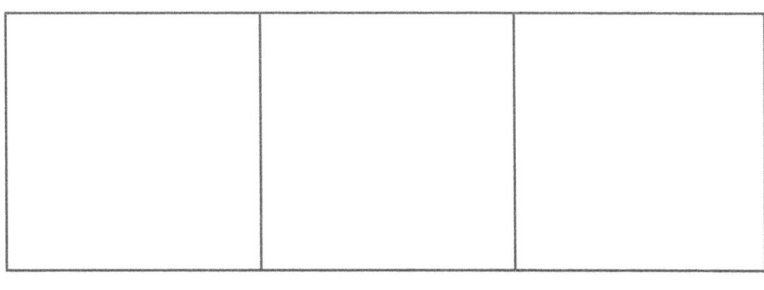

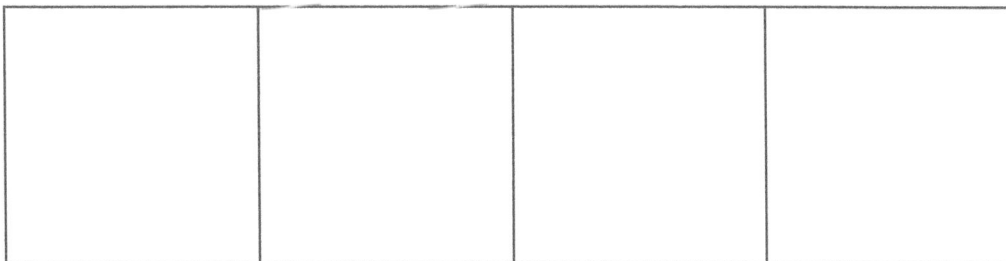

MANIPULATION

Manipulating phonemes in words may involve adding a sound, deleting a sound or substituting a sound or sounds in words.

This is a particularly difficult skill in the oral stages of literacy and the teacher may elect to leave the teaching of this skill until a later time, such as when the student has had exposure to the letters (graphemes) of the alphabet.

Students are often exposed to the written symbols and letter names, and have little knowledge of the sound structure of the alphabetical principle on which our language is based. This being the case, students' skills for encoding (spelling) and decoding (reading) may be jeopardised without the auditory discrimination skills that are practised with phonological and phonemic awareness activities.

After exposure to a wide range of phonological and phonemic awareness activities, and the written symbols have been introduced, these letters may act as a visual scaffold for the sounds that need to be held in the short term memory in order that the student can add, delete, rearrange or substitute sounds.

The following sequence of skills may be undertaken primarily as oral exercises and again at a later stage when the student is familiar with the letters of the alphabet. This is particularly relevant for the latter stages in the manipulation process.

STAGES OF SOUND MANIPULATION

1. Deletion of first syllable in a word. Example: Tig-er without the 'tig'.
2. Deletion of second syllable in a word. Example: Paint-er without the 'er'.
3. Deletion of first sound in a word. Example: Omit the first sound 'r' in rat, to make 'at'.
4. Substitution of first sound in a word. Example: Replace the first sound 'c' in cat with 'p' to make 'pat'.
5. Substitution of final sound in a word. Example: Replace the final sound 't' in mat with 'p' to make 'map'.
6. Substitution of medial (middle) vowel. Example: Replace the middle sound 'a' in 'cat' with 'o' to make 'cot'.
7. Deletion of first sound in a consonant blend. Example: Say 'slap' without the 's'(lap).
8. Deletion of final consonant in a consonant blend. Example: Say 'soft' without the 't'(sof).
9. Deletion of the second consonant in a final consonant blend. Example: Say 'blend' without the 'n' (bled).

It may be helpful to use tokens to represent each sound when doing manipulation exercises, especially if written letters have not been introduced. The tokens represent a more tangible illustration of the presence of a sound.

When doing deletion exercises, either deletion of a beginning or final sound, the appropriate token is removed. and in a similar manner, when a letter is substituted this letter may be replaced with a different coloured token to illustrate a change of sound and where this change has occurred.

The use of a different colour token for each different sound may be beneficial.

DELETION OF FIRST/SECOND SYLLABLE IN A WORD
(Suggested lesson plan)

STUDENT OUTCOME
The student is encouraged to successfully identify and retain in their short-term memory, two individual phonemes that are then blended to form a word.

When deleting the second syllable use the plan in reverse.

METHOD
Teacher: We are going to listen to two parts of a word'. The teacher then demonstrates the two parts by placing two tokens or clapping twice as a two-syllable word such as 'tractor' is spoken. One token is placed as 'trac' is spoken and the second token is placed as 'tor' is spoken. The first counter is now removed.

Teacher: 'I have now taken the first 'trac' part, which part is left?

Student: 'tor' is left.

Practise with as many words as you can. (Pictures from the Syllable Counting Section, using compound words and two syllabic words.

EVALUATION
The student is proficient in the skill when he/she demonstrates the ability to recognise both syllables of a word and say the second syllable.

SKILL
Deleting the onset of a two-syllable word whilst retaining the rime section in the short term memory, thus enabling the student to articulate the second syllable.

SUGGESTED WORDS

Family and friends' names:
Row/an, Stu/art, Col/leen, Thom/as, No/la, Lu/cy, Tris/ten, Pe/ter, Lau/ra, Al/ice, Ber/yl, Aud/rey, Ar/nold, Di/anne, Me/gan, Don/na, Lyn/ette.

Fruits and vegetables:
ap/ple, or/ange, cab/bage, lem/on, let/tuce, pump/kin, mel/on, beet/root.

Towns and cities:
Mel/bourne, Syd/ney, Dar/win, Gee/long, Red/bank, Gis/borne, Mal/don, Bir/chip.

Things:
pen/cil, rub/ber, rul/er, cray/on, foot/ball, jump/er, scoot/er, racq/uet, mar/bles.

Occupations:
Build/er, doct/or, art/ist, butch/er, pi/lot, driv/er, ty/pist, ba/ker, clean/er, sail/or, plumb/er.

DELETION OF INITIAL SOUND IN A WORD
(Suggested lesson plan)

STUDENT OUTCOME
The student is encouraged to correctly identify a sequence of sounds, and then delete the initial sound to form a new word.

METHOD

Explain to the student that you are going to play a word game.

Teacher: 'I am going to say a word, 'rat', and if I leave off the 'r' sound, I only have 'at' left.

Continue the deletion exercises with words suggested in the lists shown on the following page, (or make words of your own).

EVALUATION

The student is able to retain in the short memory the initial sound of the given word, then omit that initial sound to make a new word.

SKILL

Deletion of an initial sound to form a new word.

WORD LIST FOR THE DELETION OF THE INITIAL SOUND

ORIGINAL WORD	NEW WORD
cat	at
bat	at
sat	at
rat	at
fat	at
hat	at
pat	at
fan	an
pan	an
can	an
man	an
ran	an
tan	an
van	an
sit	it
lit	it
bit	it

ORIGINAL WORD	NEW WORD
fit	it
hit	it
pit	it
rest	est
best	est
log	og
bus	us
jog	og
sand	and
band	and
hand	and
land	and
stop	top
stone	tone
wink	ink
spot	pot
seat	eat

SUBSTITION OF INITIAL SOUND
(Suggested lesson plan)

STUDENT OUTCOME
The student is encouraged to correctly identify a sequence of sounds, and then delete the initial sound to form a new word.

METHOD

Explain to the student that you are going to play a word game.

Teacher: 'I am going to say a word, 'rat', and if I leave off the 'r' sound, I only have 'at' left.

Continue the deletion exercises with words suggested in the lists shown on the following page, (or make words of your own).

EVALUATION

The student is able to retain in the short memory the initial sound of the given word, then omit that initial sound to make a new word.

SKILL

Deletion of an initial sound to form a new word.

WORD LIST FOR THE DELETION OF THE INITIAL SOUND

ORIGINAL WORD	NEW WORD
cat	at
bat	at
sat	at
rat	at
fat	at
hat	at
pat	at
fan	an
pan	an
can	an
man	an
ran	an
tan	an
van	an
sit	it
lit	it
bit	it

ORIGINAL WORD	NEW WORD
fit	it
hit	it
pit	it
rest	est
best	est
log	og
bus	us
jog	og
sand	and
band	and
hand	and
land	and
stop	top
stone	tone
wink	ink
spot	pot
seat	eat

SKILL

Substituting the initial sound in a word and replacing it with a different sound to make a new word. For the purpose of these exercises some words may be non (dictionary) words

SUBSTITION OF INITIAL SOUND
(Suggested lesson plan)

STUDENT OUTCOME
The student can correctly identify and blend a sequence of sounds to make a word, and then substitute the final sound to form a new word.

METHOD
Explain to the student that we are going to play another word game but this time we are going to change the last sound.

Teacher: 'I am going to say the word, 'cat', and I want you to listen carefully because I am going to make a new word. If I leave off the 't' sound and say a 'p' sound I have made a new word, 'cap'.

Continue the substitution exercises with words suggested in the following lists, (or make words of your own).

EVALUATION
Competency in the skill is demonstrated when the student can substitute the final sound with an alternate sound, (given by the teacher) and then make a new word.

SKILL
Retain in the short-term memory the correct sequence of sounds, and then replace the original final sound with a different sound to make a new word.

WORD LIST FOR THE SUBSTITUTION OF THE INITIAL SOUND

ORIGINAL WORD	NEW WORD
bed (replace 'd' with 'n')	Ben
bet	bed
Ben	Bess
Get	guess (ges)
cap	can
cap	cat
can	cap
cab	can
bit	bid
Ben	bet
big	bin
pat	pan
pig	pin
pop	pot
tot	top
dot	dog
cot	cod
cup	cut
did	dig
dug	dull

SUBSTITUTION OF MEDIAL SOUND
(Suggested lesson plan)

STUDENT OUTCOME
The student can correctly identify and blend a sequence of sounds to make a word, and then substitute the medial (middle) sound to form a new word.

METHOD
Explain to the student that we are going to play another word game but this time we are going to change the middle sound.

Teacher: 'I am going to say the word, "man", and I want you to listen carefully because I am going to make a new word by putting a new sound in the middle of this word'.

The teacher now places three tokens as the word 'man' is spoken.

Teacher: Now I am going to take the 'a' sound away and put in 'e' (a different coloured token is placed to replace the 'a'). This sound is 'e'. What is the new word?

Continue the substitution exercises with words suggested in the following lists, (or make words of your own).

EVALUATION
The student is competent in this skill when he/she can delete the medial sound, then substitute a given sound and finally articulate the new word.

SKILL
Recognise a new word after the substitution of the medial sound in a three-sounded word.

WORD LIST FOR THE SUBSTITUTION OF THE MEDIAL SOUND

ORIGINAL WORD	NEW WORD
bat	bit
bad	bid
bit	but
bet	but
cot	cat
dog	dig
dig	dug
fan	fin
fit	fat
get	got
hut	hat
hip	hop

ORIGINAL WORD	NEW WORD
bin	bun
bag	bog
bun	bin
bog	big
cut	cot
dim	dam
dull	doll
fox	fix
fin	fun
hit	hot
him	hum
hem	ham

SUBSTITION OF MEDIAL SOUND
(Suggested lesson plan)

STUDENT OUTCOME
The student can correctly identify a word by, blending and retaining a sequence of sounds and then omitting the first sound to make a new word.

METHOD
It may be helpful to continue the use of tokens when doing these exercises as they serve to illustrate the number and position of each sound in the target word.

Teacher: 'I am going to say the word, "man", and I want you to listen carefully because I am going to make a new word by putting a new sound in the middle of this word'.

The teacher now places three tokens as the word 'man' is spoken.

Teacher: Now I am going to take the 'a' sound away and put in 'e' (a different coloured token is placed to replace the 'a'). This sound is 'e'. What is the new word?

Continue the substitution exercises with words suggested in the following lists, (or make words of your own).

EVALUATION
The student is competent in this skill when he/she can delete the medial sound, then substitute a given sound and finally articulate the new word.

SKILL
Recognise a new word after the substitution of the medial sound in a three-sounded word.

WORD LIST FOR THE SUBSTITUTION OF THE MEDIAL SOUND

ORIGINAL WORD	NEW WORD
blend	lend
brick	Rick
spoke	poke
clean	lean
crumb	rum
pray	Ray
cloud	loud
play	lay
snap	nap
block	lock
sting	ting

ORIGINAL WORD	NEW WORD
bring	ring
slick	lick
grain	rain
snail	nail
train	rain
glad	lad
black	lack
small	mall
Fred	red
clean	lean
slip	lip

DELETION OF SECOND SOUND IN AN INITIAL CONSONANT BLEND

The previous lesson plan for the deletion of the first sound in an initial consonant blend may be adapted for the deletion of the second consonant sound in the following words.

ORIGINAL WORD	NEW WORD	ORIGINAL WORD	NEW WORD
blend	bend	bring	bing
slick	sick	spoke	soak
grain	gain	clean	keen
snail	sail	crumb	come
pray	pay	black	back
play	pay	small	Saul
snap	sap	Fred	fed
block	Bock	sting	sing
slip	sip	stand	sand

DELETION OF FINAL SOUND IN A CONSONANT BLEND
(Suggested lesson plan)

STUDENT OUTCOME
The student can correctly identify, blend and retain a sequence of sounds and then omit the final sound to make a new word.

METHOD
It may be helpful to continue the use of tokens when doing these exercises as they serve to illustrate the number and position of each sound in the target word.

Teacher: 'I am going to say the word, "best", and I want you to listen carefully because I am going to make a new word by leaving off the last sound, 't'.

The teacher now places the four tokens as the word 'best' is spoken.

Teacher: 'Now I am going to take the 'k' away. What is the new word'?

Student: 'Bes'.

Continue the deletion exercises with words suggested in the following lists, (or make words of your own).

EVALUATION
The student is competent in this skill when he/she can delete the medial sound, then substitute a given sound and finally articulate the new word.

SKILL
Recognise a new word after the substitution of the medial sound in a three-sounded word.

WORD LIST FOR THE DELETION OF THE FINAL SOUND IN A CONSONANT BLEND

ORIGINAL WORD	NEW WORD
test	Tes
fund	fun
mend	men
bent	Ben
pant	pan
bump	bum
lamp	lamb (lam)
belt	bell (bel)
tilt	till (til)
gust	Gus
milk	mill

ORIGINAL WORD	NEW WORD
bend	Ben
lend	Len
wind	win
lent	Len
tent	ten
damp	dam
hump	hum
felt	fell (fel)
melt	Mel
mist	miss (mis)
jumped	jump

DELETION OF FIRST SOUND IN AN INITIAL CONSONANT BLEND

This is a diffi cult concept for students who are in the formative phase of learning the basic reading skills, especially if written symbols (letters) have not been introduced, therefore it may be a skill that is not introduced until students have had further practice with, and revision of, the previously taught manipulation skills of segmenting and blending.

DELETION OF FINAL SOUND IN A CONSONANT BLEND
(Suggested lesson plan)

STUDENT OUTCOME
The student can correctly identify, blend, retain in the correct sequence, the sounds of a word and to then omit the second last sound of the word to make a new word.

METHOD
It may still be helpful to continue the use of tokens when doing these exercises as they serve to illustrate the number and position of each sound in the target word.

Teacher: 'I am going to say the word, "hand", and I want you to listen carefully because I am going to make a new word by leaving off the second last sound, that is, the sound just before the last sound 'd.

The teacher now places the four tokens as the word 'hand' is broken into its individual sounds h–a–n–d.

Teacher: 'Now I am going to take the 'n' away. What is the new word?'

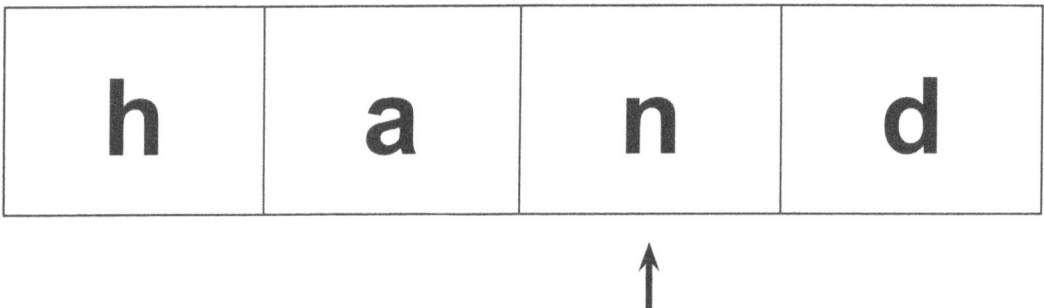

Student Replies: 'Had'.

Continue the deletion exercises with words suggested in the following lists, (or make words of your own).

EVALUATION
the student is competent in this deletion skill when he/she can articulate the new word after deleting the first sound of a final consonant blend.

SKILL
Recognise a new word after the deletion of the first sound in a final consonant blend.

WORD LIST FOR THE DELETION OF THE FIRST SOUND IN A FINAL CONSONANT BLEND

ORIGINAL WORD	NEW WORD	ORIGINAL WORD	NEW WORD
lost	lot	spend	sped
band	bad	bend	bed
hand	had	sand	sad
lend	led	send	said (sed)
bent	bet	hint	hit
lent	let	lint	lit
pant	pat	sent	set
went	wet	camp	cap
lamp	lap	pump	pup
belt	bet	melt	met
desk	deck	fist	fit
list	lit	gust	gut
just	jut	must	mutt
rust	rut	mist	mitt
left	let	milk	Mik
silk	sick (sik)	next	net

NOTES